A Cornerstone Book

In His Own (w)Rite
Michael R. Poll

A Cornerstone Book
Published by Cornerstone Book Publishers

Cornerstone Book Publishers
Hot Springs Village, AR

First Cornerstone Edition - 2011
Second Cornerstone Edition - 2014
Third Cornerstone Edition - 2022

www.cornerstonepublishers.com

ISBN: 978-1-61342-157-4

Table of Contents

Introduction

What is Freemasonry? Well, it pretty much depends on who you ask. In the 35+ years I have been a Mason, I have visited quite a few lodges. No two have been exactly alike. Lodges seem to develop personalities of their own, much like people. Some are relaxed and laid back, and some are more formal. Some are very healthy with work going on all the time, and some, sadly, are on life support. But, in each lodge where I've had a chance to speak with individual members, they have expressed true caring about their membership. Sure, it does not mean the same thing to each of them. The one in the khaki pants and bright Hawaiian shirt with the donut in his hand might view the reason for his membership differently than the one in the tuxedo with the white gloves and a glass of wine, but so what? Who said Masonry must mean the same thing to everyone?

The common denominator in all lodges is that Masonry lifts Masons up a bit more from where they started. Not everyone is a philosopher, and not everyone will draw the deeper meanings from the Masonic ritual, but we all can benefit from being told to try and be better than we are today. Sure, few (if any) live up to the deepest teachings of Freemasonry, but is our goal perfection or the striving for it? I believe that if we just try to live as Masonry teaches, recognizing that we all fail from time to time, then we are doing what is expected of us. Masonry is not for everyone, and we cannot expect that it will, in any way, satisfy someone who is just not Masonic material. But, for those who are touched by Masonry, no matter what they are wearing, eating, or the state of their lodge, they feel deeply about being a Mason. It is important to them, and no matter how much or little they know of the ritual or its deeper teachings, it is of value to them.

Our Masonic history is important to us. We must have a record of who we are and from where we come. But this is not really a Masonic history book. I have, however, a deep interest in the early history of the Scottish Rite. I have this interest because we have such sketchy accounts of the early days of it. While this is not a Masonic history book, I have included some history papers exploring aspects of Scottish Rite history that we might not see explored very often. This is also not a book of philosophy. But we can all benefit from the life lessons that Masonry teaches. I try to teach Masonry in a way that applies to everyone so that we all can see and experience its lessons. With this in mind, I've included papers and lectures with aspects of Masonic teachings that apply to us all.

So, that's what we have here; a collection of history and "Masonic life" papers – with some other bits I find helpful or noteworthy. If this book gives you just a moment to think about yourself and your role in Masonry, or gives you any cause to think of ways to improve yourself, then I consider this book a worthwhile endeavor.

Be happy, enjoy life, and make each beautiful moment count.

Michael R. Poll
Fall, 2011

In His Own (w)Rite

Fluid Masonry: The Art of Change

WHEN WE BOIL FREEMASONRY DOWN to its most basic element, we find a very simple message: "make yourself better." Such a statement can, however, be likened to the phrase "be happy." It sounds easy enough, but how do you do it? How do you know when you are "better?" What *is* "better?" What seems to be an uncomplicated message becomes difficult to put into practice, even to understand. Such is the nature of symbolism.

We can start on the path of symbolic understanding by looking at nature. If you look at a beautiful mountain stream, you can find more than beauty. You can find illusion (often, the guardian of symbolism). Flowing water moves around a large rock in the stream. The illusion is that the rock is the master. What we believe to be the truth is the sight of the water yielding to the rock and being forced to flow around it. We see this and accept it as truth. Our error is that we determined "the truth" before we gathered all the facts. In time, gentle, flowing water can reduce the largest stone to a pebble. The rock is not the master. One lesson to learn is that what we see, hear, feel, and believe might well prove to be something other than fact. We must train ourselves to withhold judgment.

In Freemasonry, a subtle lesson is taught early on by putting us in a position where we cannot depend on what we can see. We are forced to depend on others for guidance. We are also forced to use senses other than those upon which we would typically rely. We must change in order to adapt to this new situation. The illusion is that we have been handicapped and deprived of receiving the full benefit that would have been afforded us if we had complete use of all of our senses. But the illusion masks the fact that we are forced to adapt to our condition precisely because we have been placed in such a state. We simply can't act or perform on our own. We need guidance.

The three degrees in Craft Masonry are often said to represent the three stages of human life: youth, adulthood, and old age. How do we progress through these stages? We change. As children, we play, grow, and learn. As adults, we put into practice what we have learned, and in old age, we impart to others what we have learned. In each stage, we change in body and mind. It is the normal way of life. What would be abnormal is if no change took place.

Let's look again at the water and the rock. The gentle, flowing water cannot and does not break the rock by direct force. Water changes its direction and flows around the rock; in doing so, it also gradually affects change in the rock. The gentle pressures of the water force the rock to give way and reduce itself in size. The rock is not the master, after all. Change is one of the unavoidable facts of all existence. Any attempt to avoid change only results in unnatural waste of energy.

The lessons of Masonry are such that we must study them with a child's open and willing mind. In certain aspects of our teachings, we might remember we are told that bringing "innovations" into the body of Masonry is unacceptable. An innovation is a change. Are we being told that we cannot or should not change? Not at all.

As individuals, we change every day of our lives. We grow older, which brings physical and mental changes. We have no choice in these types of changes. We also have the option to make free-will choices in our lives. We might opt to eat a more healthful diet, to exercise, or in some way improve our lives. There are countless changes that we can choose. We also might make the decision *not* to make any free-will changes. It is our choice as individuals.

But when we speak of innovations in Masonry, we are speaking of something quite different. The innovations that are made in Masonry should never be the choice of any single individual. Changes should be the collective will of the membership. In Masonry, it is the lodge, not the Worshipful Master, who decides the direction to be taken. The Worshipful Master only steers the ship in the desired direction. In our Grand Lodges, we see change every year. We see resolutions presented and voted on. It is rare that a Grand Lodge will see no change whatsoever in its nature after a Grand Lodge session. Change is normal. Change is expected.

In Masonry, the changes we see in its nature often mirror the changes we see in wider society. Freemasons are part of society, and we interact with others on a daily basis. It would be unnatural for us to be social outcasts. If we look back at Masonry 50 or 100 years ago, or even longer, we see that the nature of Masonry matched that of society in both simple matters of dress and deep social or philosophical issues. Even today, we see social differences in Masonry depending on the location of the lodge and its membership.

In a large city, you might see lodge members dressing in a different manner than you would see in a small town. One is not right and the other wrong; they are just simple differences in the social norms of the areas.

When we look at society and speak of a large nation, it would be uninformed not to realize that society's concepts of what is acceptable and unacceptable vary from community to community. The overall social structure of a large area allows for change and variations within smaller areas. Speed limits might change from one place to another, as well as many other community-based laws, but where will you find murder legal? Society as a whole has limits as to what are acceptable standards.

Because Grand Lodges are sovereign and free to pass the rules and laws of their liking, it would seem highly improbable that you would find two Grand Lodges with exactly the same set of governing laws. If one Grand Lodge changed its laws to require all members to wear tuxedos to lodge, it might draw a level of interest from some other Grand Lodges, but that would be about it. If the same Grand Lodge removed the Volume of Sacred Law from its altars, then not only would this attract the attention of other Grand Lodges, but they would view this Grand Lodge as moving outside of what is considered acceptable. Breaking of fraternal relations with this jurisdiction might follow. By the same turn, if most Grand Lodges adopted a particular policy that they felt was extremely important, then those few Grand Lodges not adopting the policy might also be viewed as unacceptable or out of step.

Change is not the enemy of Masonry. Just as the water in a stream changes direction as it flows in and around various obstacles, so should we recognize that change is not only inevitable but is in our best interest. In a storm, it is the strong, unyielding tree, not the flexible blade of grass, which is in the most danger of breaking.

MAGVS
V.E.V.

Albert Pike's Address Before The Grand Consistory of Louisiana

I believe readily that you did not want the office, but the office wanted you.

- Charles Laffon de Ladébat to Albert Pike [1]

THE PASSAGE OF YEARS can sometimes elevate a historical figure into a legend. This is not always beneficial when a study of the individual is desired. Historical figures can be examined, and their actions understood from a human perspective. A legend, however, can often take on near supernatural qualities, and the whole of their activities are sometimes not expected to be understood, explained, or completely recounted. Such is, at times, the case with Albert Pike. It is often difficult to imagine Albert Pike as *a* player (rather than as *the* player) in American Scottish Rite events of the 1800s. The monumental mark that Pike left on the Southern Jurisdiction can mask the fact that his influence was not always as profound as it was in his later years. Regardless of his many accomplishments, there was a time when Illustrious Brother Pike was but an inexperienced yet promising Mason with a blank book before him upon which it was unknown exactly what would be written.

This address, the first ever given by Pike as the presiding officer of a Scottish Rite body, gives us a rare look at the early Albert Pike. While in his later years, many viewed Pike as a true Master of the Scottish Rite, this address clearly calls into notice his immaturity in the Rite, and he asks for "lenient judgment" upon his "short-comings." In his address, Pike is clearly humble and seems sincerely appreciative of his election. He also notes that his election to the position of Commander in Chief was politic in nature and due to "circumstances that surround us." What could have caused a political election of the untried Albert Pike as the presiding officer of the Grand Consistory of Louisiana? Let's look at the "circumstances."

The Turmoil that was Louisiana Masonry

Just seven years prior to Pike's assuming the leadership of the Grand Consistory of Louisiana, the whole of Louisiana Masonry underwent a dramatic shift in direction, leadership, and character. The once French-dominated Grand Lodge of Louisiana became "American" in nature. This shift mirrored the cultural changes taking place in New Orleans and other French areas of the state. Louisiana was founded as a French colony. Even after the territory became a state in 1812, the French influence was the dominant force, especially in the city of New Orleans. Not only was the Grand Lodge of Louisiana a French-speaking body, but so were the five lodges that created it. Louisiana was the most "foreign" Grand Lodge (as well as state) in the U.S. Over time, many did not view this as

Creole Cottage in the French Quarter

an acceptable situation. There was a desire to "be like everyone else."

By the 1830s, Louisiana Masonry, as well as the whole of the Louisiana culture, began feeling intense pressure to become "more American." With many, this was not a welcome change. Bitter disputes and unyielding divisions developed that culminated in actual violent clashes between the "Creoles" and "Americans" in the downtown New Orleans streets. The Grand Lodge was not immune to these cultural divisions, which often manifested themselves in the different rites worked by the Louisiana craft lodges. Unlike the other U.S. Grand Loges, the craft lodges in Louisiana did not only work in the Preston-Webb (York Rite) craft ritual but also in the French or Modern Rite and the Ancient and Accepted Scottish Rite craft rituals. For the most part, the French interests were championed by the craft lodges working the French or Modern ritual and A.&A.S.R. ritual. The American interests were held up by the York Rite lodges. The 1844 Constitution of the Grand Lodge of Louisiana was the last straw for many York Rite craft Masons. The new constitution officially recognized the then three rites working in Louisiana and sanctioned the creation of a "Chamber of Rites" to supervise the work of the lodges. The York position was that there should be only one recognized rite for Louisiana craft lodges (York Rite) and that the Grand Lodge should be made to conform to the same system as worked by the other U.S. Grand Lodges.

A committee of English-speaking York Rite Masons, frustrated by the lack of accommodation they perceived in the Grand Lodge, approached the Grand Lodge of Mississippi, and submitted a letter of grievance on January 23, 1845.[2] They charged the Grand Lodge of Louisiana with irregularity due to its practice and acknowledgment of various craft lodge rituals. After debate, the Grand Lodge of Mississippi agreed with the charges, declared the jurisdiction of the Grand Lodge of Louisiana as "open territory," and, by 1848, chartered seven lodges in Louisiana.[3] On March 8, 1848, these seven lodges formed a second Grand Lodge within Louisiana. John Gedge, who had spearheaded the "rebellion," was elected Grand Master of the "Louisiana Grand Lodge of Ancient York Masons." While this new Grand Lodge received recognition from only the Grand Lodge of Mississippi, its future was not nearly as bleak as it might seem.

The Grand Lodge of Louisiana was created in a manner to accommodate the needs of the lodges which organized it. The Grand Lodge was created French in nature because this was the culture of the vast majority of those living in the area of the Grand Lodge at that time. Over the years that followed, the Grand Lodge continued to exist and operate in the manner in which it was created. The majority of the membership of the lodges under the jurisdiction of the Grand Lodge, however, changed from French to American. The Grand Lodge was then viewed, by the majority, as not accommodating their wants and needs.

The Grand Lodge of Mississippi received admonitions from most U.S. Grand Lodges for their actions in Louisiana, with the majority openly condemning its activities.[4] With the exception of the Grand Lodge of Mississippi, no U.S. Grand Lodge entered into relations with the new Louisiana Grand Lodge. Regardless of their seemingly advantageous position, the Grand Lodge of Louisiana was in serious trouble.

Outside New Orleans, there were a few pockets where the French culture was strong, but much of the state was already (or was becoming) Americanized. The events surrounding the creation of the Louisiana Grand Lodge buckled the knees of the Grand Lodge because most of the lodges under this new Grand Lodge were located in the New Orleans area. New Orleans was perceived to be the largest stronghold of the French culture within the state as well as the home of the Grand Lodge. The fact that the Grand Lodge of Louisiana was overwhelmingly considered to be the "regular" Grand Lodge in Louisiana was not sufficient to overcome the internal problems stemming from the cultural divisions in New Orleans. By mid-1849, it was realized that the English-speaking lodges that had remained loyal to the Grand Lodge showed signs that continued loyalty would likely not happen. Contributing to the dilemma were divisions between the French-speaking New Orleans Masons.

Obviously, realizing that the total collapse of the Grand Lodge of Louisiana was a very real possibility, the Grand Lodge and the Louisiana Grand Lodge, A. Y.M. entered into discussions in 1849, designed to merge the two bodies.[5] That merger took place in June of 1850 with the approval of a new Constitution of the Grand Lodge of Louisiana of Free and Accepted Masons. Under the merger agreement's terms, the Louisiana Grand Lodge, A. Y.M. members declared irregular would be healed by the Grand Lodge of Louisiana, F&AM. All Lodges chartered by the Louisiana Grand Lodge, A. Y.M. (or by the Grand Lodge of Mississippi in Louisiana) would also pass under the jurisdiction of the new Grand Lodge of Louisiana, F.&A.M. John Gedge, who had served as Grand Master of the

Louisiana Grand Lodge, A. Y.M., was elected Grand Master of the new Grand Lodge of Louisiana, F.&A.M. for 1851.

While this new constitution seemed to merge the two Grand Lodges, the Grand Lodge of Louisiana was, in reality, replaced by the Louisiana Grand Lodge, AYM. All that actually remained of the old Grand Lodge was the name, organizational date of 1812, and the list of Past Grand Masters. The nature of the new Grand Lodge of Louisiana, F.&A.M. changed to match the Louisiana Grand Lodge, AYM. The "Americans" were in power.

The old Grand Lodge of Louisiana officially accommodated lodges working in the York, French or Modern, and AASR craft rituals. The French-speaking Masons believed that the two Grand Lodges merging would result in the continued recognition of lodges working in all three rites. They were horrified and outraged when the new Grand Lodge instructed all non-York Rite lodges to turn in their charters so that York Rite charters could be issued.[6] Charges of trickery abounded. Three craft lodges (Etoile Polaire, Disciples of the Masonic Senate, and Los Amigos del Orden) applied to the Supreme Council of Louisiana for relief. The Supreme Council announced that the Grand Lodge had violated an 1833 concordat between the Grand Lodge of Louisiana and the Grand Consistory of Louisiana (at that time, the highest-ranking Scottish Rite body in the State). This concordat was to assure that the Grand Lodge would provide a home for the Scottish Rite craft lodges. In return, the Scottish Rite would not charter Scottish Rite craft lodges within Louisiana. But now, with the Grand Lodge's violation of this concordat, the Supreme Council announced that it would issue charters to these lodges and allow them to pass under its jurisdiction.[7]

The French Rite Masons did not have a Grand Body from which to seek relief. The Grand Lodge had been the home of the French Rite. With no superior body for the government of the French Rite lodges, they would, ultimately, disappear from Louisiana Masonry as an identifiable force.[8]

The Setting for More Change

When we step back and attempt to look at the situation through the eyes of the participants, we can see that the Supreme Council of Louisiana taking jurisdiction over the three AASR Craft Lodges must have been just as jarring to the new Grand Lodge of Louisiana as the action of the Grand Lodge of Mississippi was to the old Grand Lodge. No one could see or know the future. The Grand Lodge of Mississippi had been a body in full, fraternal relations with the old Grand Lodge, as was the Supreme Council of Louisiana. While the Grand Lodge of Mississippi was a sister Grand Lodge, the Supreme Council of Louisiana was composed of members who were nearly all Grand Lodge officers, a good number of whom were Past Grand Masters. The Supreme Council of Louisiana was not an insignificant body. The actions of the Grand Lodge of Mississippi set into motion a series of events that led to the downfall of the old Grand Lodge of Louisiana. It was feasible for the actions of the Supreme Council of Louisiana to result in the same fate for the new Grand Lodge of Louisiana. Clearly, this situation needed to be addressed by the new Grand Lodge.

At the invitation of Grand Master John Gedge, Albert Mackey came to New Orleans in late 1851/early 1852 and established, for the Charleston Supreme Council, a Consistory of the 32°. Gedge was appointed Commander in Chief of this new consistory. The Supreme Council of Louisiana obviously charged that this was an outrageous invasion of territory.

Not only was it the fact that the Consistory was organized in New Orleans, but the manner in which it was created was the subject of severe criticism. In 1853, Charles Laffon de Ladébat wrote about the events concerning the new Grand Lodge, the Supreme Council of Louisiana, and the new Charleston Consistory in New Orleans.

> *"In presence of such despotic, anti-masonic conduct, the Scotch BB∴ resisted as men, as Masons, and formed an independent corporation under the only M∴ authority existing in Louisiana dejure et defacto. The balance remained with the new Grand Lodge, swore obedience to her, through indifference rather than from conviction. Soon after this, the very same Sectarian, in his restlessness, caused Br∴ Albert G. Mackey to come from Charleston, in order to establish a Grand Consistory, exactly as if there never had existed a Supreme Council of the Scotch Rite in Louisiana. Our sectarian, after abolishing the Scotch Rite, wished to re-establish it in order to be at the head of it. This Consistory has been inaugurated; you know it M∴ W..., for you were admitted into it for proper causes. The manner in which the degrees were conferred in this spurious Consistory is and will be an eternal shame to the Br∴ who has conferred them."*[9]

While we can only speculate as to the events which might have caused this "eternal shame" statement, it is evident that the creation of the Charleston consistory in New Orleans fanned the flames of emotion and deeply angered the already frustrated New Orleans Scottish Rite Masons. But what could be done?

The cultural variances within New Orleans societies during the 1800s are far too complex to be explained from only a French and/or American viewpoint. New Orleans was a cosmopolitan city with layers of cultures and subcultures. The lodges under the Grand Lodge of Louisiana were not only French and English-speaking, but there were also lodges working in German, Italian, and Spanish. Like the many New Orleans neighborhoods, Masonic lodges often reflected the culture of the lodge members. Prior to 1850, the Grand Lodge maintained but minimal supervision of the lodges under its jurisdiction. As long as a lodge worked within a general Masonic framework, as defined by the Grand Lodge, the lodge was left effectively alone. For some lodges (especially in rural areas), their only contact with the Grand Lodge was when they sent in their yearly returns. Lodges were free to develop their own cultural "stamp" on both their lodge and the ritual they used. Germania Lodge No.46 was created as a German-speaking lodge receiving a York Rite charter from the Grand Lodge of Louisiana in 1844. Their 1844 ritual shows that they originally worked an eclectic ritual which may well have derived from all three rites worked in Louisiana (as well as rituals from outside the state).[10] It is very possible that the unknown author(s) of this ritual simply sat down with a number of rituals and created a unique ritual to his (or their) liking. Such independent activity was common.

The freedom extended to the lodges by the Grand Lodge may have ultimately contributed to the downfall of the French interests in Louisiana. The York Rite English-speaking

Masons may have been, by then, in the majority, but it would not have been a large majority. The non-York Rite Masons might have been able to overturn the actions of the new Grand Lodge, but they could not unify themselves and were split into unyielding factions with their own goals and agendas.

Regardless of the influence that the Supreme Council of Louisiana once had in Louisiana, the creation of the Charleston Consistory created a split that led to the demise of the Supreme Council of Louisiana as a true Masonic power.

Not only was the Supreme Council of Louisiana locked in battle with the new Grand Lodge, but it was also facing perplexing (in New Orleans) charges of irregularity – charges that it was not prepared to answer. The rapid-fire changes involving the whole of Louisiana Masonry left most of the French Masons flabbergasted and hopelessly divided as to which direction to take. It was at this time that a new "solution" was introduced that cut the divisions even deeper.

The Concordat of 1855

The Scottish Rite in New Orleans existed in what might be described as a parallel universe with the rest of the U.S. AASR Given the cultural difference between the whole of Louisiana Masonry and the rest of the U.S., the differences and detached nature of the Scottish Rite in New Orleans are understandable. With the "American invasion" of Louisiana Masonry came a forced realization that changes would have to be made in the nature of all Louisiana Masonic bodies. Exactly what changes would be necessary was the subject of heated debate.

The creation of the Mackey/Charleston Consistory in New Orleans triggered intense emotion in an already explosive environment. During this time and in this setting, a plan to "merge" the Charleston Supreme Council and Supreme Council of Louisiana was born. For those who viewed the Supreme Council of Louisiana as the only hope of preserving the French interests in New Orleans, the idea of such a plan was wholly unacceptable. The more moderate French Masons saw such a blending of the two councils as, quite possibly, the only option left. In 1860, Charles Laffon de Ladébat wrote to Albert Pike about the Concordat and explained his position.

> *"My resolution of retiring from active practice is 5 years old & more. Hear what I wrote to Mackey January 31, 1855: "When the work will be accomplished, when every thing will be in proper order & well understood, I will retire willingly & leave the management of all to more competent, but not more devoted hands". We know that the foreign influence will & must be superseded by the American element. Now the time has come & I believe that, even in Masonry, Americans must rule in America. I, a frenchman, must retire – in due time."*[11]

Not all the French Masons were willing to turn over what they viewed as their "possession" to others with different ideas, plans, and goals. When the Concordat between the two councils seemed to be inevitable, the officers and nearly half of the Active Members of the Supreme Council of Louisiana resigned or refused to take part in what they viewed as an illegal action. On January 7, 1854, the remaining Members of the council elected Charles Claiborne as the new Grand Commander, Claude Pierre Samory as Lt.

Grand Commander, and Charles Laffon de Ladébat was appointed Grand Secretary. The Concordat between the Charleston and New Orleans Supreme Councils was signed in New Orleans on February 16, 1855. The Supreme Council of Louisiana downgraded itself downward into the Grand Consistory of Louisiana, and the Grand Consistory absorbed the "Mackey" Consistory.

With the Concordat of 1855, the elimination of the French control of Louisiana Masonry was complete. The unrest, dissatisfaction, and ill feelings, however, continued to fester. James Foulhouze was the Grand Commander of the Supreme Council of Louisiana who, along with the other officers, resigned from the council rather than participate in the Concordat.

Claude Samory and Albert Mackey approached Foulhouze in the summer of 1856 to enlist his aid in healing the old wounds and to, hopefully, rebuild the AASR in New Orleans. Foulhouze was offered the office of Commander in Chief of the Grand Consistory of Louisiana and Active Membership in the Charleston Supreme Council if he would join in the rebuilding. Foulhouze declined the offers and began his efforts to reorganize the Supreme Council of Louisiana with its former officers.[12]

With James Foulhouze out of consideration, a new leader for the troubled New Orleans Scottish Rite had to be found. The choice would prove to be inspired.

Enter Albert Pike

Albert Pike

Albert Pike was an attorney by profession and a Mason of only five years when he moved his law practice to New Orleans in 1855.[13] Three years earlier, Pike received the Scottish Rite degrees up to the 32° from Albert Mackey in Charleston. Mackey saw a unique quality in Pike and recruited him to be on the ritual committee of the Charleston Supreme Council. Mackey lent Pike a collection of Scottish Rite rituals for his review and study. It was through the examination and transcription of these rituals that Pike received his first understanding of the AASR Busy with setting up his law practice and studying the rituals lent to him by Mackey, Pike did not concern himself with the momentous developments taking place in New Orleans at the time of his arrival.

One of Pike's earliest Masonic acquaintances in New Orleans was Charles Laffon de Ladébat. Over the years (even after Pike became Grand Commander), these two would maintain a "love/hate" relationship that was founded on a basic respect for each other. Ladébat was made a 33° by James Foulhouze in the Supreme Council of Louisiana on February 11, 1852, and served as its Grand Secretary at the time of the Concordat of 1855. Ladébat would later be elected an Active Member of the Charleston Supreme Council in 1859. Pike's time in New Orleans put him in close contact with many competent New Orleans 33rds who were quite capable of completing Pike's education and understanding of the AASR. Ladébat was clearly, one of Pike's early mentors.

Just as he had done with Albert Mackey, Pike greatly impressed the New Orleans Scottish Rite Masons. Pike's talent and raw abilities clearly made him a candidate for any Masonic office. The fact that Pike played no part whatsoever in the Concordat of 1855 may have made Pike even more attractive and a prime candidate for leading the Grand Consistory of Louisiana. Pike did not carry baggage with him from the Louisiana Masonic turmoil. While he was under the jurisdiction of the Charleston Supreme Council at the time of the concordat, he was not an Active Member. He played no part in any of the decisions concerning the Concordat. No one could blame Pike for any of the events. Albert Pike was the only serious candidate for leading the Grand Consistory who could be seen as potentially objective as well as extraordinarily promising. Next to James Foulhouze, no one had a better chance of appeasing the French Masons and unifying all the factions. Once the Supreme Council of Louisiana was reorganized, Pike's value to the Charleston cause was even more evident.

This address, given by Pike only four days after he received the 33°,[14] is valuable to all Scottish Rite researchers not only because it is an extremely rare piece of early Pike literature but also because of the significant information provided in it. From this address, we not only get a better feel of the early Albert Pike but also have the opportunity to develop a more detailed understanding of the momentous events that were taking place at the time Albert Pike arrived on the Scottish Rite stage. Within just two years from the time of this address, Pike would be elected an Active Member of the Southern Jurisdiction (over the apparent objections of the Grand Commander and Lt. Grand Commander)[15] and then on January 2, 1859, with the very first S.J. election of officers (a dramatic change in practice), be elected to the position of Sovereign Grand Commander.

Pike's address was ordered to be recorded in the handwritten Minutes of the Grand Consistory of Louisiana. An unknown Brother made a typed transcript of this address sometime between the 1940s and 1950s, and a copy of this transcript was acquired by this writer. The accuracy of the transcript was verified by this writer by a comparison of the transcript with the original Minutes located in the Scottish Rite Bodies of New Orleans.

ADDRESS BEFORE THE GRAND CONSISTORY OF LOUISIANA

By ALBERT PIKE

"April 29 1857

"Th ∴ Ill∴ Bros ∴ and Sublime Princes of the Royal Secret:

"I PRAY YOU TO ACCEPT my most sincere thanks and profoundest gratitude for the great and unexpected honor which you conferred upon me, when, in my absence, you selected me to fill the most honorable and very responsible station of Grand Commander of this Grand Consistory and for your present ratification of that choice. I will earnestly endeavor to have myself not wholly undeserving of your good opinion; so that, although it must now be said that when elected I was not worthy either by service or qualification, it may not hereafter be said that when I cease to serve, you repented of your selection.

"I can bring to your service, Princes, little more than good intentions, kind feelings, and a zealous devotion to the interest of Masonry of all Rites -when you find me deficient (and wherein shall I not, alas, be found, Bro ∴ ?) I entreat of you in advance lenient judgment upon my short-comings, and that you will kindly aid me with your sympathy, support and advice. For I must be ever embarrassed by the reflection that I have been by your too favorable judgment preferred to many eminent and distinguished Brethren, whose longer service and greater familiarity with the work gave them far higher claims than any I could have preferred to the post of honor and command. If I supposed that personal consideration or a belief in my superior fitness and capacity had led you to this choice, I should sink under a sense of my feebleness, not ever have succeeded in overcoming my repugnance to accept a post where so much was to be expected. But, amass that there were other reasons, which acted upon you, and made your selection seem politic and for the interest of Masonry in this Valley, reasons not personal to me, but growing out of the conditions of things and the circumstances that surrounded us. I am encouraged to hope that I may in some degree aid in attaining the result which you all desire, and that your just expectations may not be disappointed.

"I have accordingly accepted tile post which you have tendered me, and will endeavor to perform its duties. Most important private business will compel my absence for some months. I shall return as soon as practicable, and remain thereafter permanently in the city.[16]

"Should the interest of the Order at any time be likely to suffer by my temporary absence, I shall be prepared at once to surrender up my office, faintly imitating the lofty magnanimity, of which so beautiful an example has been set me by an Ill∴ Bro∴ whose genius and labors have done so much to restore the splendors of the Ancient and Accepted Rite [17] in this Valley, and whose name will not be forgotten among us, while the order of Knights Rose Croix continues to exist, or the Kadosh to war against tyranny and usurpation.

"But I shall most sensibly feel how great will be the contrast between myself, with my slender experience, and the Th∴ Ill∴ Prince and Sovereign whose place I come to take, but not fill. [18] Eminent in Masonic learning and more illustrious by long and faithful service than even by his high rank and lofty station, the new and supreme dignity recently conferred upon him was a most just and appropriate acknowledgment of his worth. This Consistory must most sensibly feel its loss, as he, Ill∴ Gr ∴ Commander, crowned and laureled with the highest honor, and with the grateful thanks and recollections of his brethren, most gracefully retires from this distinguished post, to yield it of his own choice to another. I beseech him not to withdraw from me his counsel and advice, and I pray him and our Ill∴ Bro∴ Laffon,[19] and the other eminent brethren who surround me, to aid me, to advise me, to support me in my inexperience, that, guided by them I may not despair of rendering some little service to the cause of humanity, to the cause of truth, of liberty, of philosophy, and of Masonic progress.

"My brethren, I see around me the representatives of more than one race, [20] and the disciples of more than one Masonic Rite - I rejoice at this reunion, and it gives me happy augury of the prosperity, health, and continuance of Masonry in this Valley. I am especially glad that here and in other bodies of this Rite, I see by the side of the children of the first generous and gallant settlers of Louisiana, many of another land, and who not long since for the first time passed beyond the boundaries of the York Rite.

"We are all aware, my brethren, how little among Masons of the latter Rite is known of the Ancient & Accepted Rite, and how great and general a prejudice has obtained those against it. It has been imagined that there was antagonism between the two: Scottish Masonry has been deemed almost spurious, and its degrees, at the best, no more than mere side degrees; and the York Mason who has entered into our sanctuaries has been regarded in the estimation of many, as untrue to his allegiance and disloyal.

"Those of you, my brethren, who lately have known only the York Rite, are already aware how unfounded is this prejudice, how erroneous this opinion, how chimerical these apprehensions and alarms. It shall be my study to make you more fully to know this hereafter.

"The Ancient and Accepted Rite is, when itself fully developed and understood, when itself what it should be and can be, a great, harmonious and connected system, all the degrees and lessons, embody the philosophy, the history, the morality and the essential meaning of Masonry, and are to us what the Ancient mysteries were to the initiate of Eleusis, of Egypt, and of Samothrace.

"The degrees of this Rite are commentaries on the Master's Degree, which itself is essentially the same in all Rites. They interpret instead of being at variance with that degree. They ultimately make it known to the Initiate the true word and the true meaning and inner sense of the True Word of a Mason. They teach the great doctrines that God taught the Patriarchs, and which are the foundations on which all religions repose.

"We do not undervalue symbolic Masonry, nor love it the less because we also love the Ancient & Accepted Rite, we but learn justly to value the Master's degree, by coming to understand its full meaning and to appreciate the sublime and lofty lessons which it teaches. Masonry is one everywhere and in all its Temples of whatever Rite; as it has been one in all times. Everywhere it teaches the same great lessons of morality and philosophy, or should do so, if faithful to its mission, and if its apostles are properly informed and true to the duties which it imposes on them. If anywhere it has excluded from even the inmost Sanctuaries of its Temples men of any faith who believe in Our Supreme God, Creator and Preserver of all things that become, and in the immortality of the Soul-if it has anywhere assumed the garb of religious exclusion and intolerance, of Jesuitism, of political vengeance, of Hermetic Mysticism, there most assuredly it has ceased to be Masonry.

"It would not be true to say, however, that even Scottish Masonry has adequately fulfilled or been equal to its missions. While by the irresistible influence of time, by innovations and by mutilations and corruptions of ignorance, the degrees of the York Rite have long since ceased to be what they should be, and what they were in the beginning, when they succeeded to those ancient academies of science, philosophy and morality, the mysteries; while the practice of confirming everything contained in them to the memory has by the silent lapse of time caused more and more both of ceremony and substance to be forgotten, much to be intentionally dropped, and the field of each degree to be made more and more narrow; while the true meaning of very many of their most valuable symbols have faded away and disappeared, and been replaced by commonplace, and the inventions of ignorance, and the lofty science and profound teachings, of the Ancients have too much given way to unimpressive phrases and valueless formulas, - the Scottish Rite also has not enjoyed immunity from the ravages of the biting tooth of time, universal destroyer of all human beings.

"For even here, where over the Temples of our Degrees stood perfect and complete in all the splendor and Majesty of their beautiful and harmonious proportions, we are like strangers from a far land who wander amid the shattered columns and wrecked glories of Thebes and Palmyra, and union over the ruins that track the steps of time, and over the instability of all earthly things. From many of our degrees everything has dropped out except the signs and words, and they remain half effaced and corrupted. From more, all is lost except these and some unimportant formulas; in still more, useless repetition arrives at impressiveness, but cannot renunciate us for the old science and the noble philosophy whose place it endeavors to supply. Those huge chasms have been created in the work, and the connections between the degrees have been broken; so that each has become a fragment instead of being, as at first part of one consistent, regularly progressive and harmonious whole.

"Thus it has come that of the degrees from the fourth to the thirty-second inclusive, which we retain and apply to ourselves the sounding titles, four only are habitually conferred, which all the residue remain in a great measure, and part of them altogether unknown.

"It had become so obvious that this Rite needed reformation, and that either its degrees should all be made worthy to be conferred and of value to be attained, or else those which were not so ought to be abandoned and their titles disused, that more than two years ago the Supreme Council at Charleston appointed a Committee of five Brethren to revise the whole ritual of the degrees; on which Committee I had the distinguished honor to be placed. While my Brother Laffon, both before and after he was also placed there in the stead of my Brother Samory, who to the general regret found himself compelled to decline the act.[21] While my Brother Laffon labored, more particularly on the 18th Degree, but not alone on that, I also, undertaking at first a few degrees, continued my labors during two years, until I completed a revision of all; which that it may be thoroughly examined and sanctioned, I have printed in a volume and submitted to the Supreme Council. Whether that August Body will stamp it or any part of it with its approval, is wholly unknown to me. I have endeavored to restore the effaced or faded lineament of many of the degrees to develop and elaborate the great leading idea of each, to correct the whole together as a regular series, and to make of them our harmonious and systematic whole, ascending by regular graduations to the highest moral and philosophical truth - I have endeavored to prime away all commonplaces and puerility's, all unmeaning forms and ceremonies, all absurd interpretations, and everything useless or injurious with which time and ignorance had overloaded the degrees. I have endeavored so to restore, to retouch and to supply, retaining all that was valuable and working up all the old material, as to make every degree worth to be conferred: that there should be no longer any empty tile, or barren honors in the Ancient & Accepted Rite.

"This I have attempted; but I am only too well aware that the undertaking was too great for my furios; and that what I have done will be found full of imperfections, as the work of the painter, the sculpture, the creator, and the poet ever falls short of his own ideal.

"Still I have endeavored to do somewhat; and it is my desire, at some appropriate future time, and with your consent and assistance, to confer upon some suitable candidate such of the degrees, as I have revised them, as have not been already revised by other and more competent hands.

"I congratulate you, my brethren, on the advancement and progress of the Ancient & Accepted Rite in this Valley: The Concordat by which the Supreme Jurisdiction of the Supreme Council at Charleston was acknowledged and under which the two Consistories then existing became one, laid broad and deep the strong foundations of the prosperity of our Rite. The walls of our Temple, solidly and squarely built, bid defiance to the storms of faction; and if we are true to ourselves, peace will dwell within our gates.

"And in the Realm of Masonry, if anywhere on earth, there ought to be peace and quiet and harmony. No where are schism and faction, and disunion and discontent so lamentably out of place as here. Here there should be no lust for power and no eagerness for rank or distinction. If discontented men should in this valley have established, or if any shall hereafter establish, under a foreign authority which has no jurisdiction here and act only by usurpation, any body or bodies, claiming to administer the Ancient & Accepted Rite, we shall, I think, be prepared to show that the Supreme Council at Charleston, to which we owe allegiance, is the only legitimate authority in the Rite that can exist in our country south of the River Potomac; and that the Grand Orient of France and the Supreme Council within its bosom offered against Masonic Law and Masonic Comity where they made another jurisdiction and erect their banners on the soil of Louisiana.

"It is time that this question should be receive the fullest consideration; and that the authentic history of the creation of the Grand Orient itself and of that of the Supreme Council of France, of the disputes between those two bodies and their temporary alliance should be made known to the order in the United States. Supplied with the emissary documents on both sides, it is every intention to translate them and make them public, that all may judge where is the right and where the usurpation.

"The time when fables would pass for history has gone by; and that has come when criticism and investigation will deal with the history of Masonry as with other histories, separating the truth from the error, and after reducing great pretensions to the narrowest proportions. Let us examine the history the Ancient & Accepted Rite and the Grand Orient in that spirit and by the rules and canons of sound criticism, never forgetting that courtesy, moderation, and kindness ought to inspire all Masonic discussions, hoping to find a like tone and spirit on the other side, and that those who may array themselves against us will, if Right and Truth be found with us, candidly admit it, and uniting with us acknowledge the same allegiance and so cause peace ever and ever to reign in this valley.

"My Brethren, let me impress it upon you, that there is much to do, if we would have Masonry adequately fulfill its mission. It is not sufficient merely to receive three or four of the degrees, and then, imagining the rest, to live in contented indolence, without an effort to know the high science and philosophy of the system. The time has come when one who would be truly and really be a Scottish Rite Mason must study and reflect. It shall be my earnest endeavor to aid you in penetrating to the inmost heart of Masonry and in unveiling its profound secrets, which are that light towards which all Masons at least profess to struggle, that knowledge of the True Work which is the great remuneration of a Mason's labor. But if I should fall short of the performance of this duty, be not you, my brethren, disheartened nor discouraged. Masonry must be true to itself, or it will find in numbers weakness only, and its walls will be crushed to the ground with its own might. In this intellectual and practical age. Masonry must it from merited disaster and dissolution.

"It is time for it to assume a higher ground; and here, if any where, the effort to elevate it must be made. Here, I believe, we can commence and successfully carry onward the indispensable work of reformation, that shall in time end the reign of puerility's and trivialities, and make masonry what it should be. The great teacher of moral and philosophical truth; the teacher of the primitive religion known to the first men that lived; the defender of the right of free thought, free conscience and free speech; the apostle of rational and well regulated liberty; the protector of the oppressed, the defender of the common people, the asserter of the dignity of labor and the right of the laboring man; the enemy of intolerance, fanaticism and uncharitable opinion, and of all idle and pernicious theories that arraign providence for its dispensations, and endeavor to set their notions of an abstract justice and equality above the laws by which God chooses to rule all human affairs.

"In this great work I wish your co-operation, and I ask, for myself and for those eminent brethren who are to act with me and in my place, your countenance, your assistance, and your encouragement. I am sure my brethren that I shall not ask this in vain; and that grateful, deeply grateful as I now am for your confidence and kindness, I shall be far more so, and with far greater reason, when I am allowed to surrender into your hands the trust which you have so generously confided to me."

NOTES:

1. Charles Laffon de Ladébat to Albert Pike, June 24, 1860. Archives of the Supreme Council, 33°, S.I., Washington. Photocopy in possession of the author.
2. *Report of the Committee on Foreign Correspondence of the Louisiana Grand Lodge of York Masons* (New Orleans: Cook, Young & Co., 1949), p. 5.
3. George Washington, Lafayette, Warren, Marion, Crescent City, Hiram, and Eureka.
4. *Grand Lodge of the State of Louisiana Report and Exposition (New Orleans:* I. L. Sollee, 1849), pp. 5-34.
5. James B. Scot, *Outline of the Rise and Progress of Freemasonry in Louisiana* (1873; reprint, New Orleans: Cornerstone Book Publishers, 2008), pp. 78-80.
6. Charles Laffon de Ladébat, *The Schism between the Scotch & York Rites* (1853; reprint, New Orleans: Cornerstone Book Publishers, 2008), pp. 7-8.
7. Scot, *Outline*, pp. 86-87.

8. An attempt was made in the late 1800s to revive the French Rite in New Orleans through the short lived Grand Orient of Louisiana. This body was created in 1879, but, possibly due to little support, did not last longer than ten years. See: *The Grand Orient Of Louisiana: A Short History And Catechism Of A Lost French Rite Masonic Body* (1886; reprint, New Orleans: Cornerstone Book Publishers, 2008).
9. Ladébat, *The Schism*, pp. 7-8.
10. Art de Hoyos, Introduction, *The Liturgy of Germania Lodge No.46, F&A.M.* (New Orleans: Michael R Poll, 1993).
11. Ladébat to Pike, Jun. 24,1860.
12. See: Michael R. Poll, I*n His Own (w)Rite,* (New Orleans, LA Cornerstone Book Publishers, 2011), "James Foulhouze: A Biographical Study" pp. 91-137.
13. Pike's law office was located in downtown New Orleans in a building on the riverside of Camp Street one block from Canal Street. The building no longer exists. New Orleans City Directory, 1856.
14. After the Concordat of 1855, the Active Members of the New Orleans Supreme Council were brought in as Honorary Members of the Charleston Supreme Council. As with all Honorary Members of a Supreme Council, they held the 33° but not the active office of Sovereign Grand Inspector General (S.G.I.G.). It was at this time that the Charleston Supreme Council began elevating 32° Masons to the 33° but not including the office of S.G.I.G. in their elevation. Albert Pike was one of the first 32° in the S.J. elevated to the 33° without being invested with the office of S.G.I.G. Pike would be elected an Active Member (S.G.I.G.) of the Charleston Supreme Council on March 20,1858.
15. ". ..I was not the last to devise the means of placing you at the head of the order, 1st by making you a 33rd against the will of Messrs. Furman & Honour: 2nd by vacating my office of Deputy in your favor, & twice you got in the S.C. & especially twice you were unanimously elected to the Presidency, I consider myself as having done my duty, all I could do. The lifeless council of Charleston was revived; it lives now! Only now tho!" Ladébat to Pike, Jun. 24,1860.
16. The New Orleans City Directories from 1856 unti1 1859 show that while Pike had opened a law office in New Orleans, he did not have more than a temporary home in the city. The Minutes of the Grand Consistory also reveal that he was absent for many of the meetings of the Grand Consistory. There is no record that Pike ever moved his family to New Orleans, and it is probable that he traveled between his home in Little Rock and New Orleans. One of the many boarding houses in New Orleans

would have likely been his residence during his stays in the city. Despite Pike's statement, New Orleans would never be his permanent home.

17. At the time of this address, the term *Ancient and Accepted Scottish Rite* was not in common use in the U.S. This accounts for Pike's repeated use of the older (in the U.S.) term *Ancient and Accepted Rite.*

18. Pike refers to Claude Pierre Samory. Samory was elected an Active Member of the Charleston Supreme Council on Nov. 20, 1856.

19. Charles Laffon de Ladébat.

20. Freemasonry in pre-Civil War New Orleans was reflective of the New Orleans culture of the time. Pierre Roup was the son-in-law of New Orleans Mason and Battle of New Orleans hero Dominique Youx. Roup was a member of Perseverance Lodge No.4 and sat on the lodge's building committee. He was a black Creole. While it is clear that there were more than a few black Creoles who were members of New Orleans lodges, identifying them is difficult, as ones' race was not a question asked or recorded except in notable situations. It is quite possible that there were black Creole members of the Grand Consistory of Louisiana present at the time of Pike's address. It is, likewise, possible that Pike used the word "race" in reference to the French Masons who were often considered part of the "Latin race."

21. On p. 249 of his History of the Supreme Council 33°, AASR. S.J., U:S.A (1801- 1864) (Washington: Supreme Council, 33°, 1964) Ray Baker Harris, 33°, reproduces a letter sent by Albert Mackey to Claude Samory dated Mar. 21, 1855. The letter concerns the Southern Jurisdiction's Ritual Committee and lists its members. Claude Samory is listed as the member from New Orleans and Albert Pike the member from Little Rock. Ill. Harris writes: "From all indications, the 'preparation of new copies' was in the hands of Albert Pike. He was then in New Orleans, and may have conferred with Samory in this work, but neither of them ever mentioned such a collaboration in their numerous letters written in this period." Until this address by Pike was rediscovered, it was assumed by most AASR. scholars that Samory was on this committee with Pike for a substantial period of time. Bro. Harris, assuming that Samory remained on the committee, logically wondered about the absence of communications between Pike and Samory concerning ritual matters. This address brings to light the fact that Samory retired from the committee shortly after his appointment to be replaced by Ladébat. The collaboration was not between Pike and Samory, but between Pike and Ladébat and renders the degrees written by the two and their ritual communications understandable.

Charter for the "Mackey" Consistory in New Orleans

Universi Terrarum Orbis Architectonis per Gloriam Ingentis.

ORDO AB CHAO.

From the Grand East of the Supreme Council of the Most Puissant Sovereign Grand Inspectors General of the Thirty Third degree under the C∴ C∴ of the Zenith answering to 32° 45' North Latitude: To our Illustrious, Most Valiant and Sublime Princes of the Royal Secret, Knights K-H, Illustrious Princes and Knights, Grand, Ineffable and Sublime Freemasons of all degrees, ancient and modern, over the surface of the two hemispheres: To all to whom these Letters Patent shall come, Greeting

Health, Stability and Power:

Know Ye, that we the undersigned, Sovereign Grand Inspectors General in Supreme Council of the Thirty Third degree (which Council was lawfully established in the city of Charleston, South Carolina on the 31st day of May A.D. 1801) duly congregated this 1st day of the Hebrew month Thebet in the year of the Creation 5612 corresponding to the 24th of December in the Christian Era 1851, [illegible] the ardor of our Illustrious Princes and Knights John Gedge Thrice Illustrious Grand Commander, Henry R W Hill and John Pemberton Illustrious Lieutenant Grand Commanders and P. B. Voorhies, Wm M. Perkins, N. J. Pegram, J. O. Harris, Saml R. Walker, John Claiborne, Edward Barnett, Charles Clapp, Charles F. Preher, Wm Preher, [illegible] Place, William De Kays, Geo. Arnold Holt and reposing special trust and confidence in their capacity and zeal for the Order of Freemasonry, By these presents Do Constitute them our aforesaid Princes and Knights a regular Consistory of Sublime Princes of the Royal Secret to be holden in the city of New Orleans and State of Louisiana herewith investing them with all the titles and prerogatives which any where throughout the globe, of right belong to Consistories of Sublime Princes of the Royal Secret: And we do hereby grant to them, their associates and successors full authority to assemble and exalt and perfect Princes of Jerusalem in all the intermediate degrees of Knight of the East and West, Prince of Rose Croix, Grand Pontiff, Master ad Vitam, Prussian Knight, Prince of Lebanon, Chief and Prince of the Tabernacle, Prince of Mercy, Knight of the Brazen Serpent, Commander of the Temple and Knight of the Sun.

And we the aforesaid Supreme Council do hereby constitute and appoint the Illustrious Grand Commander and his two Lieutenant Grand Commanders in the Consistory and their legal successors, our Proxies to be and appear for us or any three of us in the said Consistory, and in our name and behalf to confer the high degrees of K-H, Knight of St Andrew, Grand Enquiring Commander, and Sublime Prince of the Royal Secret upon such duly qualified Knights of the Sun as their Consistory shall deem worthy; and we invest the said Proxies with all the authority in the premises which we should have if personally present. And we do furthermore authorize the aforesaid Consistory as our special deputy to open and hold, and to grant Warrants for opening and holding Lodges of Perfection, Councils of Princes of Jerusalem and Chapters of Rose Croix in the State of Louisiana [illegible] agreeably to the Ancient Constitutions of the Order. And the aforesaid Consistory is hereby empowered to do all things which such Sublime Bodies have a right to do in either hemisphere agreeably to the Laws, Rules and Regulations of the Ancient and Accepted Rite, with this proviso, that the aforenamed Consistory do make an annual return to this Supreme Council of all persons therein admitted, specifying what degrees, the said persons have received and remitting a fee of two Dollars for every person [illegible] and the aforesaid Council shall at all times hereafter pay and cause to be paid due obedience to the [illegible] of this Supreme Council, and faithful allegiance thereto, otherwise this Warrant shall be null and void.

In testimony whereof, that full faith and credit may be given to all the lawful acts and deeds of the aforesaid Consistory of Louisiana at New Orleans, by all regularly constituted bodies throughout both hemispheres, we have granted this Warrant, and having signed the same with our own hands; have caused thereunto to be affixed the seals of our order on the day and year above written.

[illegible signature]
[illegible]
M.P. Sovereign Grand Commander

[illegible signature]
[illegible]
[illegible]

Albert G. Mackey M.D.
[illegible]
Illust. Secretary Genl. H. E.

[illegible]
[illegible]

[illegible signature]
[illegible]

[illegible signature]
[illegible]

Transcription of the charter for the "Mackey/New Orleans" Consistory

Universi Terrarum Orbis Architectoms per Gloriam Ingentis
ORDO AB CHAO

From the Grand East of the Supreme Council of the Most Puissant Sovereign Grand Inspectors General of the Thirty Third degree under the C\ C\ of the Zenith answering to 32° 45' North Latitude:
To our Illustrious, Most Valiant and Sublime Princes of the Royal Secret, Knights K-H, Illustrious Princes and Knights, Grand Ineffable and Sublime Freemasons of all degrees, ancient and modern, over the surface of the two hemispheres: To all whom these Letters Patent shall come, Greeting Health, Stability and Power:
Know ye that we the undersigned Sovereign Grand Inspectors General in Supreme Council of the Thirty Third degree (which Council was lawfully established in the city of Charleston, South Carolina on the 31st day of May A.D. 1801) duly congregated this 1st day of the Hebrew month Thebet in the year of the creation 5612 corresponding to the 24th of December in the Christian Era 1851, [not legible] the and or of our Illustrious Princes and Knights John Gedge Thrice Illustrious Grand Commander, Henry R. W. Hill and John Pemberton Illustrious Lieutenant Grand Commanders and P.B. Voorhies, Wm M. Perkins, N.J. Pegram, Wm. Prehn, L.M. Place, William DeBuys, Geo. Arnold Holt and reposing special trust and confidence in their capacity and zeal for the Order of Freemasonry. By these present, Do Constitute them our aforesaid Princes and Knights a regular Consistory of Sublime Princes of the Royal Secret to be holden in the city of New Orleans and state of Louisiana. Herewith investing them with all the titles and prerogatives which any where throughout the globe of rights belong to Consistories of Sublime Princes of the Royal Secret; And we do hereby grant to them, their as-sociates and successors full authority to assemble and exalt and perfect Princes of Jerusalem in all the intermediate degrees of Knight of the East and West, Prince of Rose Croix, Grand Pontiff, Master Ad Vitam, Prussian Knight, Prince of Lebanon, Chief and Prince of the Tabernacle, Prince of Mercy, Knight of the Brazen Serpent, Commander of the Temple and Knight of the Sun. ________________________________

And we the aforesaid Supreme Council do hereby constitute and appoint the Illustrious Grand Commander and his two Lieutenant Grand Commanders in the Consistory and their legal successors, our Proxies to be and appear for us or any three of us in the said Consistory, and in our name and behalf to confer the high degrees of K-H, Knight of St. Andrew, Grand Enquiring Commander, and Sublime Prince of the Royal Secret upon such duly qualified Knights of the Sun as their

Transcription of the charter for the "Mackey/New Orleans" Consistory

Consistory shall deem worthy; and we invest the said Proxies with all the authority in the premises which we should have if personally present. ______________________ And we do furthermore authorize the aforesaid as our special Deputy to open and hold, and grant Warrants for opening and holding Lodges of Perfection, Councils of Princes of Jerusalem and Chapters of Rose Croix in the State of Louisiana and agreeably to the Ancient Constitutions of the Order.____________ And aforesaid Consistory is hereby empowered to do all things which Sublime Bodies have a right to do in either hemisphere agreeably to the Laws, Rules and Regulations of the Ancient and Accepted Rite, with this provision, that the aforesaid Consistory do make an annual return to this Supreme Council of all persons therein admitted; specifying what degrees the said person have received and remitting a fee of two dollars for every person admitted and the aforesaid Council shall at all times hereafter pay and care to be paid due obedience to the edits of this Supreme Council, and faithful allegiance thereto, otherwise this warrant shall be null and void. ________ In testimony whereof, that full faith and credit may be given to all the lawful acts and deeds of the aforesaid Consistory of Louisiana at New Orleans, by all regularly constituted bodies throughout both hemispheres, we have granted this Warrant, and having signed the same with our own hands; have caused thereunto to be officiated the seals of our Order on the day and year above written.

J. H. Honour
R\+\, K-H\, S\P\R\S\, S\G\I\G\ 33
M\P\ Sovereign Grand Commander

James C. Norris
R\+\, K-H\, S\P\R\S\, S\G\I\G\ 33
Illust. Treasurer of the H-E-

Albert G. Mackey, M.D.
R\+\, K-H\, S\P\R\S\, S\G\I\G\ 33
Illust\Secretary of the H-E-

R\+\, K-H\, S\P\R\S\, S\G\I\G\ 33
Illust\Gd Master of Ceremonies

J.A. Quitman
R\+\, K-H\, S\P\R\S\,
Sov\G\I\G\ 33°

C.M. Furman
R\+\, K-H\, S\P\R\S\, S\G\I\G\ 33

Petition to the "Grand Consistory of the State of Louisiana" from the Worshipful Master of Western Star Lodge #61 signed on February 11, 1852, but interesting enough recommended by John Gedge and Edward Barnett, both of the "Mackey" Consistory in New Orleans.

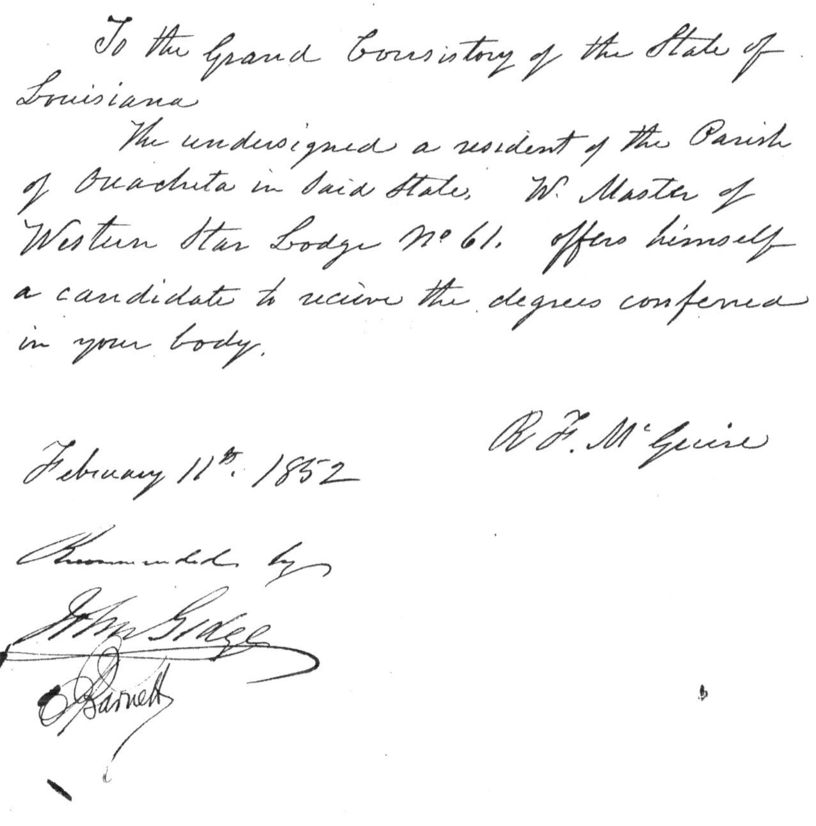

To the Grand Consistory of the State of
Louisiana
The undersigned a resident of the Parish
of Ouachita in said State, W. Master of
Western Star Lodge No 61. offers himself
a candidate to receive the degrees conferred
in your body.

R. F. McGuire

February 11th. 1852

Recommended by

John Gedge

E Barnett

MAGVS
V.E.V.

The Grand Constitutions of 1786

FEW MASONIC DOCUMENTS have been debated, praised, maligned, studied, and misunderstand more than the collection known as the Grand Constitutions of 1786. There are actually two recognized collections with that name, one known as the French version and the other as the Latin version. But what are they, why are they important, and why all the fuss about them?

The Grand Constitutions of 1786 are directly associated with the 33-degree Ancient and Accepted Scottish Rite and are its original rules and regulations. The first Scottish Rite Supreme Council was created in Charleston, South Carolina, on May 31, 1801. They claimed the Grand Constitutions as their authority to exist and as laws for their governance. The Grand Constitutions of 1786 provided the first Supreme Council with a blueprint, which guided them in the organization, structure, and management of this new system.

In the early days of the new 33-degree Scottish Rite, the Grand Constitutions were perceived to be of great importance to the young Supreme Council but were of no value to Grand Lodges. They mostly viewed this new system as mere side degrees. For the Scottish Rite, they were central to the system's government and could also be used as evidence of legitimacy. In fact, the original Charleston Supreme Council[1] did use the Grand Constitutions as evidence of legitimacy in what would become a "Scottish Rite war" spanning most of the 19th century.

John Mitchell

John Mitchell was the first Grand Commander of the Charleston Council (i.e., the "Southern Jurisdiction"). Mitchell had been a Deputy Inspector General (25°) of an older Masonic system known as the Order of the Royal Secret, more commonly known as the Rite of Perfection. In 1807, another Deputy Inspector General, Joseph Cerneau, created bodies in New York that would evolve into a second Supreme Council in the US. The Charleston Council used the Grand Constitutions in their argument that this second supreme council was illegal and irregular. In 1813, Emanuel De La Motta, an Active Member of the Charleston Council, traveled to New York and – with or without the knowledge or authorization of the Charleston Council – created a second supreme council in New York on August 23, 1813, intending to replace the Cerneau creation. This council would become the Northern Masonic Jurisdiction.

Interestingly enough, the Northern Masonic Jurisdiction (NMJ) and the Southern Jurisdiction (SJ) have historically differed as to which version of the Grand Constitutions they acknowledge. The NMJ accepted the French version, and the SJ the Latin version. But why should there be different versions of a document that would seem to be crucial to the Scottish Rite? What and where is the original?

The Grand Constitutions of 1786 contain 18 Articles, or rules, which were reported to be approved and signed in

Joseph Cerneau

Berlin by Frederic the Great on May 1, 1786. The original document has never been seen or known to exist. When the Charleston Supreme Council demanded that Cerneau produce documentation showing it was authorized to exist, the Cerneau Council produced nothing. The Charleston Council labeled the Cerneau Council irregular. When the Cerneau Council demanded that the Charleston Council give proof that they were authorized to exist, the Charleston Council pointed only to its copy of the Grand Constitutions of 1786. The Cerneau Council dismissed this document as a forgery and accused the rival group of hypocrisy. The Cerneau Council claimed it had the same right and authority to exist as did the Charleston Council and that they demanded that the standards for legitimacy should be the same for all.

Another claim made by the Charleston Council was that any additional supreme council created in the United States needed its approval, which it did *not* give to Cerneau. This requirement appears nowhere in the Grand Constitutions.

So, who, if anyone, was correct? Is it possible that the Grand Constitutions of 1786 *were* a forgery and never approved by Frederic? Let's have a look at the two versions of the Grand Constitutions of 1786. Of the French version, Albert Pike says:

If I were satisfied that there never were any other Constitutions than those contained in the French version, I should not hesitate to admit that they were a clumsy forgery, and that there was nothing in the world to prove them authentic.[2]

Those are very strong words! But why would Pike write such a powerful denunciation of this French version? Past SJ Sovereign Grand Commander Henry Clausen explains:

Pike's [Latin] version is obviously a truer copy of the original because it supplies omissions and corrections that were apparent in the French version.

Following are a few examples from Pike's pen showing the disparity between the French and the Latin versions:

The French Constitutions neither provide for nor describe any Jewel or Cordon of the Degree. The Seal is described as 'a large BLACK Eagle with two heads, the beak of gold, the wings displayed, and holding in its claws a naked sword; upon a ribbon displayed below is written DUES MEUMQUE JUS, and above the Eagle, SUPREME COUNCIL OF THE 33rd DEGREE. [Official Bulletin, Vol. V, No. 2, p. 548]

The French Constitutions provide for one Council of the Degree in each Nation or Kingdom in Europe; for two in the United States of America; for one in the British West Indies; and one in the French West India Islands. But none is provided for Canada; none for the Province of Louisiana, or the Spanish Possessions in North America; and none for South America. [Official Bulletin, Vol. VII, No. 1, p. 486]

Their Article VI provides that 'the power of the Supreme Council does not interfere in any Degree below the 17th and Article VII that only Councils or individuals above the Grand Council of Princes of Jerusalem may bring their appeal to the Supreme Council. This was necessary, in 1801, at Charleston, to prevent hostility on the part of the Grand Lodge of Perfection and Grand Council of Princes of Jerusalem, then and theretofore existing in South Carolina. Why was it necessary in 1786, in Prussia, where no Lodge of Perfection or Council of Princes of Jerusalem existed? [Ibid., p. 487] The fees for the 33rd Degree and for the Patent of it are expressed to be payable, not in German, but in French coin. [Ibid., p. 487] [3]

Pike's rational and categorical reproof of the French version makes it difficult to understand how one could, with any understanding of Pike's argument and its implications, reasonably defend the French version. Yet, this is the very version that the NMJ accepts. Why? Even more interesting is the fact that Pike himself used the French version to support his position in a Masonic debate. In the 1860s, the Supreme Councils of the NMJ and SJ entered into a debate over territory. Josiah Drummond, the Grand Commander of the NMJ, and Albert Pike, the Grand Commander of the SJ, debated jurisdictional questions over certain states.

Drummond wrote to Pike in 1868:

I hold that under the Constitutions of 1786, the Northern Jurisdiction and the Southern Jurisdiction are, in every respect and for all purposes, as distinct as if they were separate nations: that we, as well as you, derive our rights of jurisdiction from those Constitutions; that those Constitutions create two separate Jurisdictions. On the other hand, I perceive, that you have held that your Supreme Council had jurisdiction throughout North America, and that we get our territory by cession from you; and if by cession, consequently we get only such territory as you choose to cede: and as necessary, that there could have been no Supreme Council in this Jurisdiction unless you had chosen to cede us territory. [4]

How did Pike answer Drummond? He wrote (arguing the meaning of certain phrases in the French version):

I do not agree that the Constitutions created the two Jurisdictions. For the United States composed a single Jurisdiction until 1813 or 1815 and might have continued to be as such until today. The provision is restrictive – that there shall not be more than two Supreme Councils established in the United States. That is the real meaning of it; not that there shall be two. But the point is of no practical importance, and I pass it.... If Illustrious Brother Drummond were right in holding that the Northern part of the United States did not belong to the Jurisdiction of the Southern Council, prior to 1813 or 1815, but was to vest, whether it willed it or not, in a Northern Council, whenever one should be created there, a consequence which he does not foresee might follow. That hypothesis would make the Northern states to have been unoccupied territory, in which any Inspector General could establish a Supreme Council; and it might thus make legitimate the Cerneau Council and annihilate that created in 1813 or 1815 by De la Motta. It certainly would destroy the principal ground on which the legitimacy of Cerneau's Council was always impeached; to-wit, that the Council at Charleston had jurisdiction over the whole United States,

> *and that no other Council could be created anywhere in them, except with its consent.* [5]

Pike and Drummond debated the meaning of Article V of the French version, which determined the number of Supreme Councils allowed in the US. This debate resulted in Pike producing quite lengthy arguments concerning French and English grammar and the reasons for his position concerning the meaning of Article V of the French version. Pike even changed a portion of the English translation in his Grand Constitutions to reflect his opinion of the rendition.[6] In his 1868 Allocution, Pike very skillfully debated this interpretation of Article V of the French version at length, and he did likewise in his Grand Constitutions. But why should Pike bother to painstakingly argue a point concerning a version of a document that he had soundly dismissed as a "clumsy forgery"? For the sake of clearly articulating his true position, Pike should have debated the Latin version – which he claimed to be legitimate. Why didn't he? Simply put, Pike could not debate this portion of the Latin version. The same portion of Article V of the Latin version (the version Pike refers to as the "law of the Rite")[7] reads:

> *In each great nation of Europe, and in each Kingdom or Empire, there shall be but one single Supreme Council of this Degree. In all those States and Provinces, as well of the mainland as of the islands, whereof North America is composed, there shall be two Councils, one at as great a distance as may be from the other.* [8]

Pike strongly contended that the meaning of Article V (French version) was that the US was *not* required to be divided into two jurisdictions, yet that is precisely what the Latin version said – which Pike had himself published in

1859. Pike used the French version in his debate with Drummond because it was more open to individual interpretation. The undesired "consequence" that Pike claimed if Drummond's interpretation was accepted is clearly present in the Latin version – Cerneau, it seems, might have had a reason, based on the version of the Grand Constitutions accepted by the SJ, to believe that he had rightfully established his Council.

The problem for Drummond was that Pike had skillfully painted him into a tight corner with his masterful use of Drummond's preferred French version. The territorial debate ended with Drummond yielding to Pike's demands. The view held by Drummond, however, was not only based on his interpretation of Article V of the French version, but also on the "birth certificate" of the Northern Council itself, which reads in part:

> *And whereas the Grand Constitutions of the 33° specifies particularly, that there shall be two Grand & Supreme Councils of the 33d Degree for the Jurisdiction of the United States of America, one for the South and the other for the North.*[9]

It is obvious why Drummond interpreted Article V of the French version as he did. The NMJ was created on the premise that the constitutions provided for two councils in the United States. Its only contention could have been if Cerneau was not a legitimate Sovereign Grand Inspector General; after all, if he was legitimate, the Cerneau Council was perfectly legal, and the NMJ was – by its own stated reason for being created – unauthorized! Pike's opinions concerning the meaning of the original French interpretation

Frederick Dalcho

were clearly not shared by Emanuel De La Motta, who created the NMJ and was an active Member of the original Charleston Council. It is, likewise, evident why Pike's "threats" might well have been taken seriously. The only available attack that could reasonably be made on Cerneau, from the NMJ perspective, was to discredit his legitimacy as an SGIG – but great care had to be taken in this course of action as there is no reason to believe Cerneau and John Mitchell obtained the degree in any different manner.[10] To discredit Cerneau's 33° might discredit Mitchell's.

It would seem apparent that Pike was unaware of the existence of a handwritten copy of the French version of the Grand Constitutions that had been made by Frederick Dalcho, the first Lt. Grand Commander of the Charleston Council and its second Grand Commander following John Mitchell; the document was not discovered until the 20th century.[11] (This copy now resides in the Kloss Collection in the Grand Lodge Library, Netherlands, which also includes a manuscript of the Ritual of the Thirty-third Degree.) Pike boldly proclaimed the French version a fraud and offered very lucid support for his position, while having no idea of the pernicious wording of the "birth certificate" of the NMJ. An additional problem for Pike was that the Latin version was unknown before 1832. To make matters worse, it was none other than a Cerneau Council that made the Latin version available to the world.[12]

Customarily, papers discussing Joseph Cerneau include arguments concerning the Grand Constitutions of 1786. Cerneau is usually accused of acting in violation of these Constitutions. Nineteenth-century defenders of Cerneau typically argued the lack of authenticity of the Grand Constitutions, with the apparent belief that if the Grand Constitutions could be discredited, then all charges against Cerneau would likewise be dismissed. One claim that was often made was that Frederic the Great had been in very poor health at the time the Constitutions were said to be approved and that he was physically unable to have given them consent. Albert Pike went to great lengths to examine the charge that Frederic was not physically able to have executed such a document. Pike meticulously traced the reported events and laid out a detailed report on his position that it was possible for Frederic to have executed the Grand Constitutions. NMJ Scottish Rite historian Samuel Baynard writes of Pike's conclusions:

> *Though we admit that our Illustrious Brother did in a masterly manner fully convince us that Frederick on May 1, 1786, was physically able and mentally capable of drafting, signing and promulgating these Grand Constitutions, we have utterly failed to find that he discovered or pointed out to us one scintilla of evidence that Frederick actually did have aught to do with them.*[13]

Pike was obviously aware that his lengthy account did not answer the actual question of whether Frederic signed or approved the Grand Constitutions. Addressing this point in a most interesting manner, Pike writes:

> *[T]here is not one particle of proof, of any sort, circumstantial or historical or by argument from improbab-ility, that they are not genuine and authentic.*[14]

As remarkable as it sounds, Pike asks us to prove a negative. Regardless of Pike's request, Baynard continues:

> *We conclude therefore:*
>
> *1. That the Grand Constitutions were not promulgated by Frederic the Great;*
>
> *2. That they were not framed, drawn up or signed in Berlin;*
>
> *3. That there did not exist in Berlin or even France in 1786, any "Grand Supreme Universal Inspectors, in constituted Supreme Council";*
>
> *4. That the real date of the Constitutions is subsequent to 1786.*[15]

But if the Grand Constitutions are a forgery, then who forged them? The question did not escape Baynard:

> *It is only natural that the next question should be, Well, then, who did frame them? We do not know. Neither are we unduly disturbed because we do not know. We have our opinion, but it is not substantiated by any evidence that we can call positive or direct, and, therefore, we do not express it as a conclusion.*[16]

To summarize the situation, Pike pronounced the French version of the Grand Constitutions a forgery. He was debating the merits of why the Latin version should be considered legitimate. Baynard rejected *both* versions of the Grand Constitutions. Regarding the possibility that the Latin version might also be a forgery, Pike tells us:

The odious charge has been again and again repeated, that these Latin Constitutions were forged at Charleston. It is quite certain that this is not true, because the Supreme Council at Charleston never had them, until it received copies of the editions published by the Grand Commander. If they were forged anywhere, it was not at Charleston: and if anything was forged there, it was the French copy, as it afterwards appeared in the Recueil des Actes.[17]

Charleston Supreme Council

And elsewhere:

The gentlemen of South Carolina, in that day, did not commit forgery. Whatever the origin of the Grand Constitutions, they came from Europe to Charleston, and were accepted and received by the honorable gentlemen and clergymen who were of the first Supreme Council, in perfect good faith.[18]

If the Grand Constitutions are forged documents, but the original Charleston Council did not forge them, then how did they come into possession of them? Pike theorizes:

> *This very imperfect French copy, which consists merely of so many Articles, without preface, formality of enactment by any body in Power, or authentication of any sort, contains no list of the degrees, nor even the name of the Rite. It is most probable that de Grasse procured it, in or from Europe, and created the Supreme Council. By Article V of these Constitutions, it requires three persons to constitute a quorum and compose a Supreme Council; and therefore Colonel Mitchell and Dr. Dalcho alone could not have been, by themselves, such a body. Brother de Grasse intended establishing a Supreme Council at Santo*

> *Domingo for the French West India Islands; and no other person had any interest to make the Constitutions read so as to allow such a Council, except his father-in-law, Jean Baptiste Delahogue, who also resided in Charleston in 1796, 1799 and 1801, and was also a 33rd, and appointed to be Lieutenant Grand Commander for the French West Indies. It was for this reason, evidently, that neither of them was placed on the roll of members of the body at Charleston.*[19]

We now have enough material to analyze. Baynard held the opinion that the entire story of the Grand Constitutions was a fabrication. He based his opinion on the total lack of factual evidence supporting the account and the improbability of the reported events. Pike soundly denounced the French version as a fraud but held to the possibility of legitimacy for the Latin version. Pike pointed out that the original Charleston Council did not have possession or knowledge of the Latin version and had based their actions on the fraudulent French version. Pike also stated that it was Alexander de Grasse-Tilly who had brought the forged French version to Charleston, and implied that it was de Grasse-Tilly who might actually have forged them. Pike, with some indignation, rejected the possibility that Mitchell or Dalcho might have had anything to do with forgery.

There are two logical scenarios that we can explore: The first would be that Mitchell and Dalcho received the Grand Constitutions sincerely believing they were legitimate; the second would be that Mitchell and Dalcho took part in the creation of the Grand Constitutions or knew that they were a forgery.

If Mitchell and Dalcho believed that the Grand Constitutions were legitimate, we can look at the series of events with this mindset. Suppose Mitchell and Dalcho believed that they were propagating a European system created some fifteen years before the creation of the Charleston Council. In that case, they could have reasonably assumed that other Supreme Councils of the 33° existed in Europe. Clearly, the Grand Constitutions speak of such a Council in Berlin.

On August 23, 1813, John Mitchell and Frederick Dalcho wrote to Emanuel De La Motta concerning De La Motta's report to them of Cerneau. Mitchell wrote in part:

> *I am truly surprised and astonished at the conduct of the man you say is called Mr. Joseph Cerneau. No person ever had the degree but the Count de Grasse, and perhaps, but I am not sure, Mr. Delahogue.*[20]

Frederic the Great

We must stop for a moment to try and understand this comment by Mitchell. If Mitchell received a copy of the Grand Constitutions and accepted them as legitimate, how could he be so sure that no one else "had the degree"? What about the Supreme Council in Berlin cited in the Grand Constitutions? The copy of the Grand Constitutions of 1786 that Mitchell had available to him opens as follows:

> *Made and approved in the Supreme Council of the 33rd duly and lawfully established and Congregated in the Grand East of Berlin on the 1st of May Anno Lucis 5786 and of the Christian Era 1786. At which Council was present in person – His Most August Majesty, Frederic 2nd, King of Prussia, Sovereign Grand Commander.*

Was the "Supreme Council of the 33rd" in Berlin composed of members who did not have the 33rd degree? If no one else had the degree, who gave it to Mitchell? Did someone who did not possess it give it to him? Mitchell writes that de Grasse was the only person he was certain "had" the degree. (This is possibly where Pike conceived the theory that de Grasse was the one who brought the forged copy to the United States.) If no one else had the degree before de Grasse, then who gave it to de Grasse? If de Grasse gave Mitchell the 33rd at some time earlier than the creation of the Charleston Council in 1801, why does the "1802 Manifesto" (the "birth certificate" of the SJ) state that de Grasse *received* the 33rd degree from Mitchell on the "21st of February, 5802" [1802]? [21]

Let's now look at part of Frederick Dalcho's letter to De La Motta on the same day as Mitchell's letter and also concerning the new Cerneau creation. It again should be noted that the date of Dalcho's letter was *August 23, 1813*. Emanuel De La Motta established the Supreme Council for the Northern Jurisdiction 13 days earlier, on August 10, 1813. He certainly would have reported this fact to Mitchell and Dalcho in the letter that prompted their response. Dalcho wrote:

> *It is well known to those who have lawfully received the 33rd degree, that there can be but one Council in a nation or kingdom; and that the Council for the US was*

> *lawfully established in this City, May 31st, 1801; consequently any other assuming its prerogatives must be surreptitious.*[22]

What does Dalcho mean by this statement? The copy of the Grand Constitutions of 1786, which exists *in Dalcho's own hand* says, "two in the United States of America." And what of De La Motta's creation? Is there some suggestion that Dalcho might not have approved of the De La Motta Council any more than the Cerneau one? The "birth certificate" of the NMJ, created by De La Motta, states that "*there shall be two Grand & Supreme Councils of the 33d Degree for the Jurisdiction of the United States of America, one for the South and the other for the North.*"

Pike stated that the earliest known copy of the Grand Constitutions was the "forged" French version as appeared in a French Masonic publication titled *Recueil des Actes* in 1817.[23] Pike stated that Mitchell and Dalcho could not have forged the Constitutions because they were both "honorable" men and neither "the kind of man to put his hand to that kind of work." Pike also stated that it was not "probable that either of them could write Latin or French."[24] Pike theorized that de Grasse, along with his father-in-law, Jean Baptiste Delahogue, acquired or forged the French version and then, presumably, translated it into English so that Mitchell and Dalcho could understand it. Pike did not know of the handwritten Dalcho copy. But, Pike could have, by this line of reasoning, assumed that Dalcho copied it from a de Grasse or Delahogue copy which either one of them could have translated from French into English for Dalcho. Could this be the copy that was used to fool Mitchell and Dalcho? We learn from past SJ Grand Historian Ray Baker Harris that the Delahogue documents in the Kloss Collection are *"an undoubted copy of the Thirty-Third Degree and the Constitution, Statutes and Regulations, in use in Charleston in 1801-1802 when the Supreme Council was established."*[25]

Harris also tells us:

This assumption is further confirmed by a manuscript copy of the same in English, entirely in the handwriting of Frederick Dalcho. It is the English equivalent of Delahogue's French copy. It is believed to have been the Charleston copy from which Delahogue made his translation into French.[26]

Delahogue made his translation *into French*? But Pike said that the oldest known copy of the Grand Constitutions was the forged French language version. In a reproof of this version, Pike rigidly defended Mitchell and Dalcho based on his position that this forged copy came into their hands, presumably through de Grasse and/or Delahouge, and they simply accepted it as legitimate. The "French version" would have had to have been translated from *French into English*, not the other way around for Pike's argument to be sound. Is there some support for Harris' position that the French Delahouge copy was made from the English Dalcho copy? Yes. Harris tells us that the Delahogue copy of the Grand Constitutions carries the note:

translated from the English by me [Delahogue].[27]

For Pike's theory to be correct, de Grasse would have translated his forged French Constitutions into English for Mitchell and Dalcho. Dalcho would then have copied that English translation into his own hand. Then, we are asked to believe that de Grasse's father-in-law did not make a French-to-French copy of the Constitutions from de Grasse's copy, but instead used Dalcho's English copy to translate it back into French for his own personal copy. That makes no sense at all! Why would Delahogue go to all that trouble if his son-in-law possessed the original French version?

This writer is wholly in agreement with Samuel Baynard in his rejection of the legitimacy of the Grand Constitutions. Likewise, there is little room to argue the perfectly logical assessment Albert Pike made of the French version of the Grand Constitutions. Pike clearly did not realize that what he so soundly proved to be a "clumsy forgery" came directly from the hand of Frederick Dalcho.

In the absence of any other reasonable explanation, we must conclude that John Mitchell and Frederick Dalcho fabricated the story of the Grand Constitutions of 1786, either in whole or in part. We cannot, as Pike suggested, attempt to prove or disprove a negative. We also cannot embrace fanciful theories that make the story end as we might wish. The course of events simply does not make sense if we take the position that Mitchell and Dalcho received the Grand Constitutions, accepted them as legitimate, and created the Charleston Council. The known facts simply do not support such conclusions.

This writer holds the opinion that Mitchell, Dalcho, and possibly a few others held reasonable concern regarding the failing and chaotic state of the Order of the Royal Secret (or Rite of Perfection). To bring "order" to the "chaos," the new 33-degree AASR system was created. The "cream of the crop" of the degrees and rituals were selected for this new system. It was an inspired creation for which, one can imagine, a concern developed over whether it would be accepted by the whole of Freemasonry. A royal endorsement would add value to any new Masonic system, and one attached to a set of governing laws might bestow greater value.

If we examine the situation from the standpoint that the Charleston Council received the Constitutions and accepted them as legitimate, we arrive at one contradiction after another. If, however, we consider the entire story and creation came from the Charleston Council, a very logical scenario develops. It is this writer's conclusion that the original Charleston Council was created alongside a set of governing laws attributed to Frederic II. This writer has not seen one scrap of sound evidence to support the position that Frederic approved – or even knew of – any Grand Constitutions in Berlin on May 1, 1786. There is, however, abundant evidence to attribute the creation of the Constitutions to the original members of the Charleston Council.

It has been more than 200 years since the creation of the Charleston Council. The value and worth of the AASR is well proven. It is clear this Masonic system is of tremendous importance to the whole of Masonry, and it is not a disservice to acknowledge all its history. The creators of the AASR were human, after all, and humans sometimes make mistakes in judgment.

NOTES:

1. Today, the official name is "*The Supreme Council [Mother Council of the World] of the Inspectors General Knights Commander of the House of the Temple*

of Solomon of the Thirty-third degree of the Ancient and Accepted Scottish Rite of Freemasonry of the Southern Jurisdiction of the United States of America" — but more commonly known simply as the "*Southern Jurisdiction.*"
2. Albert Pike, *The Grand Constitutions of Freemasonry* (New York: The Supreme Council, 33° Southern Jurisdiction, USA, 1872), 282-283.
3. Henry C. Clausen, *Authentics of Fundamental Law for Scottish Rite Freemasonry* (San Diego: The Supreme Council, 33° Southern Jurisdiction, USA, 1979), 9-10.
4. *Transactions of the Supreme Council of the 33D for the Southern Jurisdiction of the United States* (New York: Masonic Publishing Company, 1869), 19.
5. Ibid., 22-23.
6. Pike, *The Grand Constitutions of Freemasonry* 289. Pike altered the English translation of the French version of Article five to: "...but two in the United States of America..." to emphasize his point concerning his interpretation of the meaning of this phrase.
7. Ibid., 283.
8. Albert Pike, *The True Secret Institutes and Fundamental Bases of the Order of Ancient Free and Associated Masons* and the *Grand Constitutions of the Ancient Accepted Scottish Rite of the Year 1786.* (New Orleans: The Supreme Council, 33° Southern Jurisdiction, USA 1859), 163-165. In Pike's 1872 (A.M. 5632) *The Grand Constitutions of Freemasonry,* he altered the original translation of the Latin version to read as follows: "*In each great nation of Europe, and in each Kingdom or Empire, there shall be a single Council of the said degree. In the States and Provinces, as well on the Continent as in the Islands, whereof North America consists, there will be two Councils, one at as great a distance from the other as may be possible.*" Pike, the master linguist, replaced the word "shall" with "will" in his 1872 edition, which, while having the same meaning, was not such an obvious problem to inattentive readers. The edited edition carries the note, "Re-translated from the Latin by Albert Pike, 33°, Sov. Gr. Commander. A.M., 5632" p. 213. Pike maintained the accuracy of his 1859 translation, at least, until 1868, as the questioned portion of Article Five is reproduced in the 1868 *Transactions* of the SC SJ exactly as they appeared in the 1859 translation on page 28.
9. Samuel Harrison Baynard, Jr., *History of the Supreme Council, 33° Ancient and Accepted Scottish Rite Northern Masonic Jurisdiction of the United States of America and its Antecedents* (Boston: The Supreme Council, 33° Northern Masonic Jurisdiction, USA, 1938), Vol. I, 175-179. This quotation is taken from the facsimile reproduction of the 1813 "birth certificate" for the Northern Jurisdiction (reproduced on page 176). In addition to the facsimile is a printed transcript of the "birth certificate" provided to us by

Ill. Brother Baynard. Interestingly, the printed transcription omits a number of words and phrases that appear in the facsimile. The phrase, for example, "one for the South and one for the North" (line 26 of the facsimile), does not appear in the printed transcription.

10. The question of where and when John Mitchell and Joseph Cerneau received their 33rd degrees did not escape the notice of Masonic researchers. In the case of Cerneau, he is usually dismissed quickly due to the total lack of evidence that anyone ever actually gave him the 33°. Emanuel de la Motta, upon first meeting Cerneau, attempted to obtain certain information about Cerneau's 33° including having a look at his Patent, but was unable to satisfy himself in any way (see: Charles S. Lobingier, *The Supreme Council 33°* [Louisville, Kentucky: The Supreme Council, 33°, SJ., 1964], p. 102.). But what of John Mitchell? There has never been a Patent discovered showing that Mitchell received the 33° from anyone. We know that Mitchell gave Dalcho the 33° as a Patent for this event exists. Mitchell was the first Sovereign Grand Commander of the SJ, so how did he receive the 33°? Who gave it to him? Prior to Mitchell's role in the creation of the AASR, he was a Deputy Inspector General (25°) of the so-called "*Rite of Perfection.*" We often see those senior to Mitchell in this system being credited with giving him the 33° (usually Barend Spitzer). How could a 25° Mason from the "*Rite of Perfection*" give someone the 33° of the AASR? They are two different systems and two different degrees. Logic must come into play at some point. We can also see an account of some "unknown" Prussian or German giving him the degree, with Mitchell signing an obligation for it *in French.* (See: Baynard, *History of the Supreme Council, 33°*, Vol. 1, p. 89.) If someone gave Mitchell the 33°, who gave it to *him*? Why didn't this unknown SGIG play a role in the creation of the Charleston Council? Since this unknown SGIG was senior to Mitchell, why wasn't *he* the first Charleston Sovereign Grand Commander? The questions can go on forever. One thing we must never do is judge past events by today's standards. How we do things today, may not have been the norm in the past. We can find evidence of an old practice that might shed some light on the Mitchell/Cerneau 33° question. Evidence exists (see: Henry Wilson Coil, *Coil's Masonic Encyclopedia* [New York: Macoy Pub. & Masonic Supply Co., 1961], p. 121 and Pike, *The Grand Constitutions of Freemasonry*, p. 117.) that a Deputy Inspector General of the old so-called "*Rite of Perfection*" (as were both Mitchell and Cerneau) could "slide over" to the 32° of the new 33 degree AASR. In addition, if a 32° of the AASR was the senior (or only) 32° in an unoccupied area, he could advance himself to (or assume) the 33° of the AASR in order to give the

degree to others and create a Supreme Council. Both Mitchell and Cerneau gave the 33° to others and created supreme councils. Regardless of the historic disapproval of Cerneau, it is possible that according to the custom of that time, he received the 33° in the same manner as Mitchell. A sound argument could be made that he was just as legitimate an SGIG as Mitchell.

11. See: R. Baker Harris and James D. Carter, *History of the Supreme Council, 33° (1801-1861)* (Washington, DC: The Supreme Council, 33° Southern Jurisdiction, USA, 1964), 98.
12. Ibid., 216.
13. Baynard, *History of the Supreme Council, 33°*, 101.
14. Pike, *The Grand Constitutions of Freemasonry,* 170.
15. Baynard, *History of the Supreme Council, 33°*, 115.
16. Ibid., 116.
17. Pike, *The Grand Constitutions of Freemasonry* 126.
18. Ibid., 195.
19. Ibid., 134.
20. Harris/Carter, *History of the Supreme Council, 33° (1801-1861)*, 117.
21. Ibid., 323.
22. Ibid., 118.
23. Pike, *The Grand Constitutions of Freemasonry*, 126.
24. Ibid., 134.
25. Harris/Carter, *History of the Supreme Council, 33° (1801-1861)*, 92.
26. Ibid., 92.
27. Ibid., 92.

The "White Cap"

EVER HEAR THE EXPRESSION, "He's an Honorary 33rd"? It's common to hear, but ... it's just not correct.

There are two "parts" to the 33rd Degree – the office (SGIG) and the degree (33rd). A "White Cap" has received the 33rd and final degree of the AASR, but they are *Honorary* Sovereign Grand Inspectors General (also termed "*Inspector General Honorary* or *IGH*). The honorary aspect applies to the *office* of SGIG, not their degree. A "White Cap" is not an Active or voting Member of a supreme council.

Confusing? Let's look at some of the history.

Things were a little different when our 33-degree system was created. The final degree was patterned upon the final degree of the old "Order of the Royal Secret" (aka: "Rite of Perfection"). This means that the final degree was not only a degree but also an office held by the one receiving the degree. Those who received the degree performed certain duties which could only be performed by those who held both the degree and the office.

The early AASR was governed by a set of rules laid down in a collection of documents known as the "Grand Constitutions of 1786." These Constitutions (the history of which is not exactly relevant for this discussion) were accepted as the law of the Rite by the early Charleston

Supreme Council. These constitutions gave specific instructions on the organization and membership of a supreme council. A supreme council would consist of nine Members who held the 33rd Degree (in the SJ, that number would expand to 33 Members under the administration of Albert Pike). The degree name, as well as the name of this office, was "Sovereign Grand Inspector General." In the very early days, all those who held the 33rd Degree were also Active Members (voting members) of a supreme council.

It was not too long after the creation of the U.S. supreme councils that Members of one jurisdiction began moving their residence into the jurisdiction of other supreme councils. We can find cases of these "sojourning" 33rds being received in other supreme councils and cases of some being made "Honorary" Members of their host supreme council. These honorary memberships were more of a "tip of the hat" and recognition of rank. While a recognition, the title carried no voting privileges or official duties.

In the 1850s, a dramatic innovation took place in the SJ. Albert Pike was one of the first 32nds to be elevated to the 33rd degree but *not* receive the office of Sovereign Grand Inspector General. The office and degree became split. It was required for one to have received the degree to hold the office of SGIG to, but no longer would those who were elected to receive the degree automatically hold the office.

The Supreme Council under Albert Pike also created two honor investitures. One was for the 32nds and commonly known as "Knight Commander Court of Honor (KCCH)," and the second was for the 33rds (IGH) and became known as "Grand Cross Court of Honor (GC)." Pike had become aware of an older honor investiture in the Scottish Rite bodies in New Orleans for both 32nds and 33rds by the name of the "Ceremony of the Fiery Heart." It is possible that this older ceremony provided the inspiration for the KCCH and GC investitures.

It is unfortunate that we so often see the "White Cap" included with the honor investitures of the AASR. The "Knight Commander Court of Honor" and the "Grand Cross Court of Honor" are honor investitures given to those who have received the 32nd or 33rd. These two honor investitures are not degrees and including the 33rd in with them might be one source of confusion regarding the nature of the 33rd degree itself.

The 33rd degree is the final degree of the AASR. It is certainly an honor to be found worthy of receiving the degree (most do not receive it), but it is not an honor investiture.

MAGVS
V.E.V.

Integrity in Masonry

Lecture given at the 18th District Lodge, New Orleans, Louisiana August 22, 2011

THANK YOU FOR INVITING ME to talk this evening. As the Worshipful Master mentioned, I had the pleasure of serving the 18th District as District Grand Lecturer during the mid to late 1980s. My final year was in 1990. That opportunity to serve put me in contact with some extraordinary brothers, some of them, sadly, are no longer with us. One such brother was Worshipful Brother Irl Fergerson.

Back in the '80s, Bro. Fergerson was the Chairman of the Permanent Committee on Work. In my early days in Masonry, I would go to the old Masonic Temple Building and enjoy afternoons listening to him and learning the work. He was, without a doubt, one of the finest ritualists I had ever met. He not only knew the ritual forward and backwards but also inside and out. But it was his style of teaching that most impressed me. I well remember him tapping loudly on his chair after he would ask a question and saying, "If I wanted a tape recorder, I would go to the store and buy one! I don't want you to give me words properly strung together; I want you to tell me what those words mean!"

Brother Fergerson was not satisfied with anyone only correctly knowing the ritual; he wanted them to understand the philosophy being taught. In this manner of teaching, new doors began to open for me in my Masonic education. I found in our ritual something of a blueprint for living a virtuous life, a plan for inner growth and development. It was here that the true beauty of Freemasonry began to shine for me.

Learning the ritual from Brother Fergerson allowed me to study and learn the profound moral philosophy embedded in our teachings. I learned symbolic lessons that not only assisted me in my Masonic life but in all aspects of my life – inside or out of Masonry. I learned how to treat others, properly examine my own life, my flaws, and positive points, how to properly interact with others, and what is truly the most important aspects of life. I learned life lessons. One of those lessons, integrity, is the subject of tonight's talk.

Around the world, there are many different types of Freemasonry. By that, I mean the rituals that are used and practiced. While the words and activities of the craft degrees in the different rites vary, sometimes quite a bit, one common thread that runs through all of the various rites and rituals is the legend of Hiram. Now, before I say anything else, I have to throw in a disclaimer of sorts. Some time back, I heard that a jurisdiction was thinking about removing the legend of Hiram from their ritual. As surprising as that information was, the reason behind their idea was even more remarkable. I was told that they wanted to remove this aspect of the ritual because they could not establish that the legend of Hiram was a factual historical event. I was stunned. It is a symbolic story, a lesson. It is completely irrelevant if the story of Hiram is fact or fiction. We are not teaching a history class. The story is used as a vehicle to deliver lessons of virtue and morality. The lessons that are taught are what is important, not the factual nature of the story used to present the lessons.

So, with that disclaimer (and the understanding that I am not making statements of historical facts concerning the Hiramic Legend), I will continue with the story. The story takes place at the time of the building of King Solomon's Temple. We are taught that a great many operative Masons worked on the construction of the Temple. These Masons were guided in their work by three Grand Masters: King Solomon, King Hiram of Tyre, and the lead architect, Hiram Abif. At some point, the three Grand Masters realized that a number of the craftsmen were performing their duties at such a high skill level that it entitled them to special recognition. These craftsmen would be elevated to Master Craftsmen.

Now, in today's Freemasonry, if we receive a degree, an office, or a position of importance, we're honored by that advancement. But, in reality, it means very little outside our Masonic life. Our Freemasonry is Speculative Freemasonry, and it is something we do outside our family life and livelihood. This was not the same with the old Operative Freemasons. Freemasonry *was* their livelihood. It was how they fed their family and paid their bills. Being advanced to the rank of Master was a significant accomplishment. Not only did it mean an elevation in their social status, but it also meant a considerable pay increase. This advancement was a very important event in their life.

When the news of the pending advancements was made known, we can assume that considerable excitement and interest developed. It is because of the importance of these advancements to the lives of those receiving them that some concerns among the Grand Masters developed. It seemed reasonable to put into place some sort of security measure so that individuals of low moral character could not assume rank to which they were not entitled. It was decided that a secret word would be given to all new Masters of the Craft so that they could prove their rank by the possession of this word. As a further security measure, it was decided that this word would not be given out to anyone unless all three Grand Masters were present and agreed to the investiture.

The story goes on that three craftsmen obviously realized that they would likely not be elevated to a higher rank, and they were unhappy about it. They wanted this advancement – badly. So much did they want this advancement that they hatched a plan to steal this "secret word," move to another area, and live their lives pretending to hold a rank that they did not earn. They caught one of the Grand Masters alone and demanded that he tell them the secret word. When he refused, they roughed him up a bit. When the Grand Master still refused to give them the word, they became desperate. They made it clear to him that they were going to leave with either the word or him dead. At this point, the Grand Master had a choice. He could give them what they wanted, or he could risk death. Clearly, he took them seriously as his final words reflect an acknowledgment of what he knew would happen, "Of my life, you may deprive me; of my integrity, never!"

Think about what happened for a minute. There is something that I have been taught since childhood, and, most likely, you have also been taught. It is that if I am ever in a situation where someone threatens my life in a robbery attempt, I should give them whatever they want. Why didn't he? I was taught that nothing I have on me was worth risking my life. Why didn't he just give them this word, and then he could live and go on with his life?

The lesson of integrity is involved not because of a robbery attempt but because of an agreement. This Grand Master agreed that he would not give the secret word to anyone unless certain conditions were met. Had these craftsmen attempted to simply rob him of some coins, then it is reasonable that he would have freely exchanged whatever he had on him for his life. But what these men wanted was something completely different. They demanded that he violate an agreement, his word.

The Grand Master's final words need closer attention. He said, "Of my life, you may deprive me ..." What does that mean? He clearly recognized that he was not in control of their actions. He could not make them spare his life or do anything at all. Taking his life was something that they would either do or not do, and he had no control whatsoever over their actions. The only thing over which he had total control was his actions. They could take his life, but they could not take this word from him. He could only give it, and that would be by his choice.

The Grand Master needed to determine what was of true value to him. He knew that we all live and die, but he also knew that how we live is up to us. To be robbed of some money is no dishonor, but what of violating his word? What was that worth to him? He did not agree to only give the word when certain conditions were met unless his life was threatened or only on the third Tuesday of the month if there was a full Moon. He agreed to give it only if these conditions were met. Period. If he gave the word to anyone and those conditions were not met, then he would be violating his word. It did not matter if they offered him money, threatened him, or anything else. He would either keep his word or break it.

In life, we can gain or lose material things. Because of the twists and turns in life, we can amass great wealth or lose everything we own. Many things can happen to us because we are either in the right or wrong places. But either we have integrity and honor, or we do not. We have it because it is our choice, and we lose it by the same choice. Material things can be taken away from us, and we might have no choice in the matter. But not our integrity. We are the only ones who have the power to give our integrity away.

The Grand Master knew that we all live and die. He also knew that all of the magnificent structures that he helped create would mean nothing if his moral foundation was made of sand – void of integrity or honor. These men had the power to take his life, but they were powerless to make him live a life without integrity. This was the point of the story – to teach a life lesson of virtue and morality, not to simply provide a historical account.

But we should not believe that the story ends here. The nature of symbolism is layered and often requires second and third looks to find deeper meanings. Just because we believe that we are acting with honor or integrity does not mean that this is the case. Let me give you an example.

A story from New Orleans in the early 1800s comes to mind. There were two men who were standing outside the St. Louis Cathedral having a friendly conversation. The two men were facing each other. One of the men felt a bit uncomfortable in his position and moved just a bit to the left to reposition himself. When the man moved over, the other man winced in pain and looked shocked. In a sharp tone, he demanded that the man return to his original position. The man who moved had no idea what the other man was talking about nor understood his strange demand. He also did not like his tone of voice. What neither man realized nor considered was that the man who moved was considerably taller than the other man. In the position he was in (unnoticed by either man), he was standing right in a place where he was blocking the sun. When he moved a bit over, the sunlight hit the shorter man right in the eyes, causing his painful reaction.

Neither man was of a mind to explain himself or ask too many questions of the other. Hot tempers took over, and a heated, nonsensical argument replaced the once-friendly conversation. And then it happened … one man exclaimed that his "honor" had become compromised, and "integrity" demanded satisfaction. A challenge to a duel was issued.

It was fortunate that neither man died in the duel, but one of them was shot in the arm. For the rest of this man's life, he lived with a useless arm as a result of the injury suffered in that duel. And for what? Honor? Integrity? One man moved a bit, and the other man had the sun in his eyes. For that, you shoot at each other?

What these men mistook for honor and integrity was pride, arrogance, and vanity. These vices were disguised as, or mistaken for, virtues. There was no loss of honor in what happened, and integrity demanded nothing in the way of a duel.

We must live our lives with honor and integrity. But we must know what a virtue is and what is a vice disguised as a virtue. It's not always as clear as we think. If anyone has ever told us that being a Mason is easy, then they misled us. There will be times when we find it most difficult to live up to our teachings. But, as we are so often told, it is the journey that is most important, not the final goal.

Writing Masonic History

"History [is] a distillation of rumour."

-Thomas Carlyle

RECENTLY, I READ SOMETHING that I found quite interesting. A Mason wrote, "Masonic history is fact and cannot be changed." I studied that line for a time and could not decide if I agreed with him. Before I could form any opinion of his thought, I would have to understand his meaning of the word "history." If he used that word to mean the actual events of the past, then I would, of course, agree with him. How could I not? Everything that any of us did yesterday is over and cannot be changed. We can't go back in time for redos. My problem was that this Mason might have used the word "history" to mean the *published accounts* of past events (Masonic history in books or papers). If this is what he meant, then I very much disagree with him.

Published accounts of Masonic history can only be considered fact when they are so proven (and even then, can be questioned). Errors of accuracy and assumptions abound in our Masonic literature. Learned historians often dramatically disagree on the "correct" interpretation of historical events when facts are lacking, and opinions are obligatory. How "history" is discovered, analyzed, and drafted is often the telltale mark of identifying a serious, objective researcher from an amateur or a political salesman with a particular Masonic organizational bias.

Typographical errors occur because we are human. Errors in dates, names, and events occur in the finest of publications and are made by the most serious and capable historians. I certainly have had my share of misspelled names, twisted dates, and various other typos, which seem to be invisible until published. When an error of fact is discovered, it should be corrected, and we should move on. Those with fragile egos or with an aversion to correction should find safer ways to spend their time. The job of a Masonic researcher is to work toward discovering and publishing the accurate history of Masonry. It is an ongoing process, and no Masonic work of history should be considered definitive. We must welcome corrections and encourage close examination of all published accounts of Masonic history. Our work can only be accepted as valid if it is capable of standing up under close examination or criticism.

Serious historians must also be ever cautious of "history with a bias." Our job is to allow the documents to "speak for themselves" and not interject personal or organizational bias into any historical study. Has this ever been done? Sadly, yes.

When we explore or write Masonic history, we must recognize that many of today's large, powerful, and very influential Masonic Bodies were quite small and fragile 100 or 200 years ago. As an example, for the first 50 to 75 years of its existence, the Supreme Council, SJUSA, existed in what can only be considered a most unstable condition. In fact, the Southern Jurisdiction (SJ) ceased to exist for a period (arguably) of about 10 to 20 years (late 1820's to mid-1840s). Much of the SJ's reported creation and early history is accepted as fact, with little to no evidence to substantiate the claims. In many areas, we are left with only the unsupported opinions and conjecture of officers of the SJ to answer many of the reasonable questions regarding its early history.

Consider also Joseph Cerneau, the first adversary of the SJ. Was he the "villain" he was (and is) portrayed to be? In just one example, Albert Mackey labels him a "Masonic charlatan."[1] Cerneau's reputation, motives, and qualifications have been denounced by the SJ from the 1800s to the present. Even Cerneau's name is today equated with "fraud."[2] Yet there is only the *opinion* of officers and supporters of the SJ to support such brutal charges against this Brother. Such unfounded character assassination is wholly unfitting Masonic works of history. There is no evidence to show that:

> a) Cerneau became a 33rd in any manner different than the first Sovereign Grand Commander of the SJ;
>
> b) Cerneau had less right than the SJ to establish his Supreme Council as provided by the Grand Constitutions of 1786, or
>
> c) that the "problem" with the Cerneau Council was anything other than the SJ simply not wanting it to exist.[3]

Masonry has no need and can support nothing but objectivity and truth in our history. We are big enough and strong enough to stand up to whatever truth there is and face that truth as Masons. We have much re-writing to do with our Masonic history, and we must weed out the "political historians." We must never again place the "good" of any Masonic organization ahead of the good of Masonry itself.

The standards of sorting fact from opinion must be standard and apply to everyone.

It is a new day and a new time. It will be an interesting ten or so years ... and it is only beginning.

NOTES:

1. Albert G. Mackey and Charles T. McClenachan, "Encyclopedia of Freemasonry" (New York: The Masonic History Company, 1915) 139.
2. "Cerneauism: This term is applied to the particular type of clandestinism and fraud which characterized the bodies set up by Joseph Cerneau and his followers beginning in 1807." Henry Wilson Coil, "Coil's Masonic Encyclopedia" (New York: Macoy Publishing & Masonic Supply Company, 1995) 125.
3. See: Michael R. Poll, *The Controversy of Joseph Cerneau: A Brief Examination* Heredom Vol. 4 (Washington, D.C.: The Scottish Rite Research Society 1995) 47-61.

The Dwellers on the Threshold

A GOOD NUMBER OF YEARS AGO, I was walking through the French Quarter of New Orleans and engaged in one of my favorite pastimes – exploring used bookshops. In one old shop, I stumbled upon a treasure. It was three large boxes filled with old *The New Age* magazines (today, it's called, *The Scottish Rite Journal*) from around 1907 through the 1970s. It was an almost entirely intact collection. They were selling the lot for $40.00! I tried to hide my excitement out of fear that they would quadruple the price, paid the man, and loaded up my car. When I returned home, I began to wade through my acquisition. What a haul! I laughed at the very early editions with piano, shotgun, and even insurance company ads. What great period pieces! Over the next few weeks, I studied and examined all aspects of the publications.

In my collection of old *The New Age* magazines, I could see something of a snapshot of the times and changes that took place. The publication itself changed over time from colorful cover images with each issue having a unique cover to standard covers of one design for each issue. The size of the publication changed as well from a large format to a smaller, almost pocket format. What was also interesting was to see the changes in the types of articles published. The WWI and WWII issues, of course, reflected news of the terrible war years and contained a number of patriotic articles. But it was the years from around 1915 to the early 1920s that really caught my attention. These were the true esoteric years of *The*

New Age. These editions stand out from all the other years (even to the present) by the nature of the articles published. The Rosicrucian, alchemical, and metaphysical aspects were all represented in force in these editions. It was a dream come true for those interested in the deeper Mystic Arts of Freemasonry. And, like many who are workers in these Arts, a number of the authors employed pseudonyms. One such author identified himself as "Mysticus." His papers were of a nature that deeply impressed me. I began to search through each edition to discover and drink in his words. This was an enlightened Brother.

In the June 1920 edition of *The New Age* magazine, I came upon an article by "Mysticus" that especially caught my attention. It was not exactly the main subject of the article that caught me, but what seemed to be more of "side" information. The article was part of a series that "Mysticus" had written entitled "A Corner of the Library." This segment was "Collectors of Occult and Magical Books." In his article, "Mysticus" tells of a little group that existed in Washington, D.C. He writes:

> *Washington city is a well-known center of scientific and philosophical inquiry. Some twenty-one years ago there existed in the capital a little band of independent thinkers of which I was a member. We were students of philosophy, folk-lore, symbolism, occultism and psychic research, and we called ourselves, jokingly, "Dwellers on the Threshold," a title borrowed from Bulwer-Lytton's strange Rosicrucian story, "Zanoni." Some of us were professed idealists, followers of Plato and his school, while others bordered on materialism, and offered up their devotions at the shrines of Spencer, Comte, and Haeckel. But, all of us, I think, were earnest seekers after truth and*

> *open to conviction on any question. The leader of this group was Dr. [Leroy M.] Taylor, a man of wealth and a prodigious collector of occult literature. We met at his house every Saturday night to discuss problems in philosophy and religion, particularly those bordering on the mystical, for which the doctor had a decided penchant.*

Other members of this little group included Dr. Saram R. Ellison, 33°, Frank H. Cushing, Judge Thomas H. Caswell, 33°, Sovereign Grand Commander of the Supreme Council, SJUSA, and even Harry Houdini. What I would personally give to have been able to sit in on one of these meetings!

But who was this "Mysticus"? I had to find out. I sent letters to the then editor of *The Scottish Rite Journal*, Bro. John Boettjer, as well as others at the House of the Temple who I had the pleasure of knowing – the Grand Historian, Bill Fox, Sr., the Grand Archivist, Dick Matthews, and the extremely helpful and knowledgeable Librarian, Mrs. Inge Baum. All searched their records and compared notes on the possible identity of this prolific and mysterious writer. No one could turn up anything. Mrs. Baum was particularly taken with this mystery, and we exchanged a number of letters (yes, paper letters, not emails) on the subject. She had located all of his writings published in *The New Age* but had no clue who might have been the man behind the name. Then, all at once, the mystery seemed to be solved … in a mysterious way.

One evening, I was reading a copy of Manly Hall's, *The Phoenix*. In a section he had written on Albert Pike, there was a quote that hit me right between the eyes. I knew I had read those words before. I knew it was from one of the pieces written by "Mysticus" and published in *The New Age*. To be sure, I pulled out the edition with the story and compared the two. It was the exact quote. *But,* credit for the quote was not given to "Mysticus;" it was given to "Henry R. Evans." BINGO! Was this the real name of "Mysticus"? I began looking through my copies of *The New Age* and found the name "Henry R. Evans, 33°" on quite a few pieces. In fact (and to my great surprise!), Henry R. Evans was the ***Editor*** of *The New Age*. I sent all this information to Mrs. Baum, and in no time, she answered me with even more information. She sent me the whole file on Bro. Evans from the House of the Temple archives and included a letter Evans wrote to the then Sovereign Grand Commander admitting that he was "Mysticus." Mystery solved. Or did it only lead to more mysteries? How did Manly P. Hall know that "Mysticus" was Henry R. Evans?

In looking through my collection of books by Manly P. Hall (I had quite a collection of them), I saw credit given to Evans a number of times, including in the Hall classic, *The Secret Teachings of All Ages.* But I was able to find no information at all as to how they knew each other. It could not have been a case of Hall simply reading something he liked written by Evans in some publication and using it. He had to have known that Evans was "Mysticus" (apparently, not everyone did) in order to give credit to Evans and not "Mysticus." Could Hall have been a very young member of "The Dwellers on the Threshold"? Who knows? How long did this group exist and meet? Who knows? All that we can do right now is guess.

There is an old thought that water seeks its own level. Enlightened spirits bump into each other because they are going in the same direction. Little groups of Masons meet in private "clubs" like the "Dwellers on the Threshold" because their interests draw them together. If we look around, we might see such groups meeting today in many more areas than we realize – maybe not all discussing the same thing, but matters of interest to them. And I'm sure we will find at the core of each group a Masonic spark that feeds the perpetual search for knowledge and Light.

I'm glad that I found those old boxes of *The New Age* magazines. I'm glad that I was able to learn of "Mysticus" and explore his thoughts, ideas, and his mystery. I'm also very glad to continually discover the cord connecting Masons in their journey to enlightenment.

A
B
C
MAGVS
V.E.V.

Down the Path of Proper Research

A YOUNG MAN DECIDED TO WRITE a family history and began the task of putting all of the family members into their historical places. Two long-deceased brothers, who had been his much older cousins, presented him with an interesting dilemma. The younger brother was the type of man anyone would want in their family history. He was a wealthy attorney and a pillar of his community. He sat on the board of directors of the local bank and the art museum. He was a leading figure in local politics, having served as a City Councilman, and was deeply involved with a number of local charitable organizations. On the other hand, his older brother was uneducated, dirt poor, and something of the town drunk, having even spent time in the local jail for stealing chickens.

The young man pondered on the two brothers and decided that the older brother might present something of an embarrassment to the family. He decided to concentrate on the younger brother, giving as many details of his successful life as possible. The older brother was only noted in passing as the elder brother of the source of the family pride. The young man made his decision based on what he knew of the brothers and his belief that the best interests of his entire family were served by giving as little information as possible concerning the elder sibling.

An elderly aunt read the story of the two brothers and strongly protested the account. She told the young man that the father of the two brothers had died when both boys were very young. Their mother had been sick and in no condition to properly provide for the family. Fearing the boys may be taken from their mother and the family split up, the elder of the boys quit school at a very young age. He began doing whatever he could to provide for the family – including, at times, stealing chickens when they had no other way of obtaining food. The elder brother, still a boy himself, assumed the role of the father and not only provided for the family however he could but required his younger brother to remain in school to receive a proper education. Yes, the elder brother was poor, uneducated, and a chicken thief, but at his funeral, the younger brother delivered a tearful eulogy declaring that, without the sacrifices and efforts of his elder brother, he might have achieved only a fraction of his successes in life.

The young historian's account was hardly complete or accurate. In his attempt to edit history - and because he prejudged the events and family members - he deprived those who would read his work of a beautiful, factual part of family history.

Masonry has many players in its history, but not all of them have been friendly toward each other or clearly understandable in modern contexts. When a historian assumes the role of editor and chooses the relevant facts about a Mason or a body of Masons, he assumes an enormous responsibility. If one does not have a complete understanding of all events surrounding a person, place, or time, then rendering judgments without the benefit of all the facts can result in inaccurate and unfair accounts. We must recognize that some write as Masonic politicians rather than as historians. Their goal is often to paint a pleasing Masonic picture rather than present a factual and evidence-supported account of history.

The problems for our young historian in this story were two-fold: He did not possess all the needed information, and he prejudged his subjects based on incomplete facts. The task of a serious historian or researcher is often long, tedious, and mostly unrewarding. One might spend countless hours reading dusty manuscripts in dimly lit basements with the sole hope of obtaining the smallest of details. It might be far easier to grab a previously published account of a subject and paraphrase what is offered, but that ties our work to any possible errors in the previous work. We must do this work ourselves – even if other accounts exist.

Of course, there are those who believe that are no new Masonic discoveries to be made. Such naysayers are sadly mistaken. It is precisely because so much of our Masonic history is filled with incorrect assumptions – or facts based on crucial missing information, incorrect readings, or simple typographical errors – that the serious Masonic researcher has excellent opportunities for many, many new finds. We simply need to take up the cause, act responsibly, and follow the proper path.

MAGVS
V.E.V.

Dyslexia: The Gift in Disguise

"The only thing that interferes with my learning is my education."
- Albert Einstein

READ A GOOD BOOK LATELY? My wife has a true passion for reading. I often find her curled up in a lounge chair, wholly immersed in a popular or classic novel. When we first started dating, she once asked me, "Don't you enjoy reading a good book?" She looked surprised when I told her, "No, I don't enjoy reading at all." She laughed and said that I must be joking as I could almost open a public library substation with my collection of books. She could not believe me when I told her that not once in my life had I ever read a book for the sake of enjoyment. I was telling her the absolute truth. There is no enjoyment in reading for me. I read to learn something. If I want to enjoy myself, I will listen to music or watch a movie. For most of my life, I did not attempt to understand why this was the case. I simply accepted it as part of being me.

In college, my doctor put me through a series of tests and gave me a perplexing diagnosis. He said that I had dyslexia. I had never heard of dyslexia and had no idea what to expect. The doctor told me that since I was an adult, I would probably not even notice it but that the knowledge of my dyslexia might help explain some of my growing-up years. I really didn't understand what that might mean, and since he did not elaborate, I filed the information away for possible later use. That "later use" came a little over ten years ago when my then seven-year-old son was also identified as having dyslexia. I had noticed traits in him, as well as his manner of interacting with others, and methods of problem-solving, that were eerily familiar. I began a study of dyslexia. It was then that the good doctor's words and much of my painful childhood started to become clear.

The only time during my school years that was not incredibly frustrating for me was kindergarten. I imagine that this was because pretty much all that was expected was to say "please" & "thank you," not make noise in class, or beat anyone up at recess. Trouble began when more was expected. The whole of my school experience can best be summed up as a battle of wits where my teachers seemed to want *something* from me, but I could never fully get hold of exactly what it was that they wanted. The vast majority of things that were quickly understood by the class were, for the most part, nearly impossible for me to master. In contrast, the very few times that material was presented that seemed to stump the class, I was able to understand nearly before the words came out of the teacher's mouth. I could not understand why I seemed to be so very different, and different had to be bad.

Ron Davis is the author of *The Gift of Dyslexia*. It is a book that has helped me greatly in understanding dyslexia and has also provided valuable help for my son. As a child, Mr. Davis (a dyslexic) was labeled "mentally retarded" and was functionally illiterate until the age of 38. It was then that he developed a system that enabled him to teach himself to read. He went back to school and ended up earning a degree in Engineering. He was hardly retarded. In 1982, Mr. Davis and Dr. Fatima Ali, Ph.D., opened the *Reading Research Council Dyslexia Correction Center* in California, achieving great success in helping dyslexics overcome their reading difficulties.

In addition to helping dyslexics properly deal with dyslexia, Mr. Davis' work has contributed to helping the general population arrive at a better understanding of dyslexia. It has been the long-standing misunderstandings, misdiagnoses, mistreatments, and preconceived opinions of dyslexics that have caused such hardships for those with dyslexia. Regardless of how it is perceived, being dyslexic does not have to be any more of a handicap or disability than being left-handed – unless it is made so. Being left-handed is, in fact, only a difference, a different way of operating. When allowed to operate in their natural manner, left-handed students function like all other students – just using their left hands. The same is true of those with dyslexia. Dyslexia is a different way of mentally processing information. When a dyslexic child is unidentified, they can be labeled as slow, having learning/mental disabilities, or just being lazy. The child will know that *something* is wrong, both in their performance and the evaluations of them. They will not, however, be able to identify the actual problem, and the result will be great frustration and loss of self-esteem.

The most common form of dyslexia is visual dyslexia. The exact manifestations of dyslexia, however, can differ from dyslexic to dyslexic. Dyslexia will rarely manifest itself exactly the same in two individuals. A general trait of the visual dyslexic is that the thought process will be in images.

Visual dyslexics mentally manipulate images to create ideas, concepts, and thoughts. The written language is comprised of letters formed into words, which are symbols of concepts or ideas. A writer communicates his thoughts on a subject by use of letters formed into words so that the reader will understand those thoughts. Since a dyslexic thinks in images, a symbol for an image (a word) must be translated into the image it represents before the dyslexic can possess the idea. When a dyslexic reads the word "ball," they must mentally translate that symbol into an image of a ball before the symbol (word) can be understood. When dyslexia is undiagnosed, reading will be very difficult and most frustrating for a dyslexic child. Even so, most dyslexics will find methods or workarounds to their reading difficulties by the time they are adults. No dyslexic will ever enjoy reading for the sake of reading, but most will find ways to function in this medium that seems so annoying to them.

Having a dyslexic child read aloud in class presents a classic opportunity for misevaluation. Let's say that a dyslexic child is asked to read the sentence, "The ambulance has a loud siren." The dyslexic student will likely stumble at the very beginning of the sentence. The assumption will likely be made that the word "ambulance" was a problem for the child. If the word "ambulance" is considered to be a word that should be in his or her vocabulary, then the child could be evaluated as having a limited vocabulary and/or having learning disabilities. Such an evaluation fails to consider how dyslexics process information. Written words must be mentally translated into images for a dyslexic to process them. When no image can be created for a word, a mental "blank card" is replaced for the troublesome word. When reading aloud, a "blank card" will cause a stumble for a dyslexic reader.

Let's look again at the sentence that the child was asked to read. "The ambulance has a loud siren." The entire sentence creates an exciting image for most any child. Most children are thrilled at the sight of an emergency vehicle rushing down the road with lights flashing and sirens blasting. A dyslexic child should have no problem at all creating an image for an ambulance. But what image can you create for the word "the"? It was the very first word of the sentence that caused the stumble for the child, not the word "ambulance." Articles and pronouns are some of the "land mine words" for dyslexics because there are no images that can be readily created for them. Because of the manner in which non-dyslexics process information, teachers untrained in dyslexia often completely ignore words like "the" or "that," not even considering that they could be the problem. They will focus on the larger words, which, based on their personal experience, are problematic for "slow" students. The teacher will make an incorrect assumption that will lead to an incorrect evaluation of the child. The child, having no idea how the teacher arrived at her conclusion, will realize that they have no problem with the words they are accused of not understanding, but they will be unable to defend themself or explain the stumble. Frustration follows.

Undiagnosed dyslexic children, being clueless as to the nature of dyslexia or that they even have it, will not only have to figure out how to translate words, but they will have to deal with words that are untranslatable. They will also be required to solve all of these problems with no assistance whatsoever and while having to deal with the false labels of being "slow" or "lazy." And this is only when we consider the reading challenges dyslexics face. Spelling, math, and a host of other school subjects present similar problems for the dyslexic child. It is a small wonder that most all dyslexics have extremely low self-esteem. The "battle wounds" and lifelong scars received when undiagnosed dyslexics begin down the path of learning by "standard methods" usually come at an age when a child's self-esteem is developing. Dyslexics often feel that their problem is "their problem," and most have no idea that they are far from alone.

Dyslexia affects far more individuals, at varying levels, than many realize. Some of our most noted artists, scientists, businessmen, and world leaders have had dyslexia. Most dyslexics who "rise to the top" in their field do so by unconventional methods stemming from their frequently unconventional manner of learning – learning which most likely takes place in spite of, rather than because of, formal education. A few famous dyslexics include Pablo Picasso, Thomas Edison, Albert Einstein, Tom Cruise, Danny Glover, John Lennon, Winston Churchill, Nelson Rockefeller & Walt Disney. Ron Davis writes:

> *"Once as a guest on a television show, I was asked about the "positive" side of dyslexia. As part of my answer, I listed a dozen or so famous dyslexics. The hostess of the show then commented, 'Isn't it amazing that all those people could be geniuses in spite of having dyslexia.'*

"She missed the point. Their genius didn't occur in spite of their dyslexia, but because of it!

"Having dyslexia won't make every dyslexic a genius, but it is good for the self-esteem of all dyslexics to know their minds work in exactly the same way as the minds of great geniuses. It is also important for them to know that having a problem with reading, writing, spelling, or math doesn't mean they are dumb or stupid. The same mental function that produces a genius can also produce those problems."

An interesting characteristic of dyslexia is that while many of the common school lessons presented to students will be extremely difficult for the dyslexic student to master, they will excel at many of the more abstract concepts or abilities that seem to be problematic for the non-dyslexic student. It is here that the gift of dyslexia manifests itself. Most dyslexics are very analytical, creative, and capable of multi-dimensional thinking. If these gifts are not suppressed during the standard educational process, dyslexics can sometimes use the very process that gives such trouble in school to achieve what may seem to be surprising successes.

In my own case, one "surprising success" came as a result of Freemasonry. I joined right after my 21st birthday, with the "school experience" fresh in my mind. My EA initiation was, without a doubt, one of the most moving and profound experiences of my life. But after my initiation, I received news that made me wonder if my short Masonic career was over. I was told that I would be assigned an instructor to teach me what was needed to pass an exam in open Lodge. I was told this was necessary to advance to the next degree. This was about the last thing that I expected or wanted to hear. My entire school experience was a nightmare.

I could not see myself passing any sort of exam. After many delays, I finally met with my instructor. I was incredibly surprised. Had my instructor handed me a printed version of all of the work and told me that it was necessary for me to read it and then memorize it, I would likely be an EA today. The manner of "mouth to ear" verbal instruction was, however, something that was not only was possible for me to do but something at which I excelled. I flew through the work, asking and answering my own questions for my FC and MM exams. I became a certified Lodge Instructor shortly after my MM degree and, just a few years later, a District Grand Lecturer. It was not hard work that resulted in these achievements; it was the gift of my dyslexia. I simply had a gift for the memorization of things verbally presented to me.

Dyslexia is not an illness in need of a cure or a handicap that will forever deny a dyslexic the chance of living a full and rewarding life. Great advances are being made in the understanding of dyslexia as well as in providing the proper tools to educators so that dyslexic children will be able to fully realize and benefit from the educational process. In addition, a number of organizations, including the Scottish Rite, have taken on the research and proper education of dyslexia as one of their target projects.

For additional online information about dyslexia, please visit the below websites.

Davis Dyslexia Association International
http://www.dyslexia.com
The International Dyslexia Association
http://www.interdys.org
RiteCare Scottish Rite Childhood Language Program
https://scottishrite.org/philanthropy/ritecare/ritecare-srclp

James Foulhouze

A biographical study

> *Mr. Pike is altogether unknown to me, and I have never seen him, which is perhaps to be regretted, because in the event he spoke to me pursuant to the information which he has received from ill-disposed individuals, I suppose that he will be sorry for having allowed his pen to write what is neither correct nor rational.*
>
> ~ James Foulhouze, 1858.[1]

JAMES FOULHOUZE WAS, UNQUESTIONABLY, the arch-nemesis of Albert Pike in Pike's early days as Grand Commander of the Supreme Council, Southern Jurisdiction, USA. Judge James Foulhouze, former Roman Catholic priest, Sovereign Grand Inspector General of the Grand Orient of France, and Sovereign Grand Commander of the Supreme Council of Louisiana in the pre-Concordat of 1855 period, along with some of the leading New Orleans Masons, including the very respected Judge T. Wharton Collens and the powerful United States Senator Pierre Soulé, almost destroyed the Concordat between the New Orleans and Charleston Supreme Councils – a Concordat which was the breath of life to the newly reorganized Charleston Supreme Council. Who was this man who could have caused such a disturbance? *Did* he cause the disturbance, or was he, himself, swept along in a tidal wave of events?

The following is a glimpse into the life and tumultuous Masonic times of a most significant but highly controversial figure in the history of the US Scottish Rite. It is to be regretted that no photograph or likeness of Foulhouze is known to exist. It is, also, unfortunate that some areas of his life are simply lost in the mists of time.

On 1 October 1800,[2] Jacques Foulhouze was born to Michel and Jeanne Cronier Foulhouze in Riom, France. The young Foulhouze received a Catholic education at the Seminary of St. Sulpice in Paris, culminating in his ordination as a Roman Catholic priest. The Reverend James Foulhouze traveled to the United States and labored in the Diocese of Philadelphia in 1834 and 35.[3] The next record of Foulhouze in the US comes in 1835 when his name appears in a Philadelphia court records book of aliens declaring their intention to take the oath of allegiance to the United States.[4] Foulhouze would not long remain a priest nor keep his domicile in Philadelphia. An 1858 New Orleans publication contains interesting comments about Foulhouze and his possible reasons for leaving the priesthood. The comments were written by Charles Laffon de Ladébat, who will be discussed further later in this paper. Ladébat says that Foulhouze might have remained a priest had not, "Mr. (now bishop) Hughes been appointed, *in his stead,* to the important rector ship of a northern parish, to which Mr. Foulhouze was, for his long service, justly entitled."[5]

John Hughes

John Hughes (1797-1864) was the fourth bishop and first

Archbishop of the Roman Catholic Diocese of New York. Hughes served with Foulhouze in the Diocese of Philadelphia and founded the *Catholic Herald* newspaper there. Hughes was consecrated coadjutor to Bishop John Dubois of New York in 1838. He succeeded Dubois in 1842 and became Archbishop of New York in 1850.[6] Foulhouze, regardless of Ladébat's comments, could not have been affected by the 1838 Hughes appointment as the *Journal Notes* of Philadelphia Bishop Francis Kenrick record Foulhouze's faculties being suspended on 5 February 1836.[7] As with many areas of Foulhouze's life, it is unclear what could have taken place causing his separation from the priesthood. Foulhouze graduated from the highly respected Seminary of St. Sulpice in Paris. Many Catholic dioceses consider such graduates to be a highly desirable prize. The accounts of Foulhouze for that time, however, tell a different story. The records of the Archdiocese of Philadelphia,[8] while confirming that Foulhouze was a priest assigned to them, show that he had "no specific assignment."[9] This is an interesting situation. Why would the Diocese of Philadelphia not take advantage of the quality education that Foulhouze received by using his abilities and education? Foulhouze, himself, may provide the answer. In 1843, Foulhouze was asked if he had taken the vows of the priesthood, and he replied: "No, but it is true that they were given to me, against my will."[10] Regardless of the philosophical point Foulhouze was trying to make, his statement reflects that he may not have ever wholly embraced the priesthood. If Foulhouze's work reflected the same lack of interest, then it is very likely that regardless of what seminary he attended, he would not have been given assignments or appointments to higher positions. All conjecture aside, Foulhouze left the priesthood, pursued a law career, and moved to New Orleans.

Foulhouze began his law career in Philadelphia after leaving the priesthood. In 1842, he published a book in Philadelphia that reflected the same interest in philosophy that he maintained throughout his life. The 200-page work was titled, *A Philosophical Inquiry Respecting the Abolition of Capital Punishment.*[11] It is possible that Foulhouze was in New Orleans when this book was released, but it is clear that he was in New Orleans the following year. Philadelphia Bishop Francis Kenrick (Foulhouze's former superior) writes in an 1843 letter:

> *Here affairs go on smoothly but at New Orleans an infidel faction are struggling to destroy or subjugate the Episcopal authority. A fallen French priest, Foulhouze, is the editor of an impious paper,*[12] *the organ of the Marguillers. [...] The leaders in disorder are Freemasons, and they contrived to set apart a lot in the Cemetery for their Masonic brethren, and had it dedicated by a speech from their Grand Master who is a Marguiller.*[13]

The Marguillers were the wardens of the St. Louis Cathedral in New Orleans. The Grand Master that Kenrick spoke of was E. A. Canon, who was not only a Marguiller but the President of the Marguillers. The Marguillers (many of them being Masons) supervised the appointments of the priests for the St. Louis Cathedral during the early to mid-1800s. There was, of course, a great division within the congregation over Freemasons having any say in the appointment of their parish priests (regardless that these Freemasons were, themselves, Roman Catholic and members of the parish). In New Orleans, Masonry and the Roman Catholic faith were tightly intertwined in the early/mid 1800s in a love/hate relationship. It was a situation not without some hostile conflicts. An event that took place in 1842 is worth mentioning:

> *On the feast of All Saints, an incident took place in the Cathedral, which was in itself trivial, but which shows to what lengths the two factions*[14] *would go. While Father Jamey was preaching, E. A. Canon, the president of the Marguillers, entered the sanctuary by way of the choir entrance, and made a tour of the altar towards that place assigned to the president of the wardens (side opposite the door of the sacristy by which he entered). He remained there for a few minutes, but not being able to hear very well, he advanced to the balustrade of a neighboring chapel, in order to hear better. He had only heard a few words, and then decided to retire by the way he had come in, that is, behind the altar. As he was going out he was greeted by Octave de Armas, a parishioner loyal to [Bishop] Blanc, (who was also seated in the sanctuary) with the words, "Get out; you are not in your place..." Canon answered this with apparent sharp disdain and was preparing to leave when he was pushed. He was near the door of the sacristy and fell on the steps. On getting up, he heard Armas distinctly cry, "I, I alone will get rid of the wardens." The services were interrupted for about five minutes, but the Mass was soon continued and all ended calmly.*[15]

The event may have ended "calmly" at that time, but the incident was far from over. As a result of his being pushed in the St. Louis Cathedral, Canon, following typical Creole custom, sought satisfaction from Armas by means of challenging him to a duel. Armas, however, refused the challenge on the grounds that he was a Roman Catholic.[16] Friends of Canon would not let the matter drop, and charges were filed against Armas with the City Recorder. Armas was found guilty of assault. The incident reflects the growing tensions between the factions within the New Orleans Catholic community. It was in this atmosphere and, likely, through the contacts with the Marguillers that Foulhouze was introduced to Louisiana Masonry. It obviously attracted him, and he sought to be a member.

From Priest to Freemason

The Marguillers may have introduced James Foulhouze to Louisiana Masonry, but it was not his first exposure to Freemasonry itself. Foulhouze stated in 1857:

> *Being a Grandson of Free-masons, I, in my early years, conceived and entertained a desire to enter the fraternity ...* [17]

Foulhouze fulfilled that early desire by becoming a member of Los Amigos del Orden, a Spanish-speaking, New Orleans Scottish Rite Lodge.[18] Foulhouze also stated:

> *Within a year from my initiation I was made a Master Mason in the same Lodge.*[19]

Unfortunately, there are no known records of the initiation of Foulhouze nor an exact date on his initiating, passing, or raising. Foulhouze did state in his *Historical Inquiry* that he was initiated by Antonio Costa.[20] Costa was Worshipful Master of Los Amigos del Orden in 1843. An 1843 initiation followed by an 1844 raising meant rapid advancement for Foulhouze. Foulhouze was, apparently, viewed as a Mason of promise. On 14 February 1845, he was appointed Grand Translator by the Grand Lodge. The office of Grand Translator did not exist prior to Foulhouze receiving the appointment. The office was created due to the growing need for French to English and English to French translations in Grand Lodge records and documents.

In the summer of 1845 (about a year after Foulhouze became a Master Mason), Foulhouze traveled to France carrying a letter of introduction from Robert Preaux, Grand Master of the Grand Lodge of Louisiana and Active Member of the Supreme Council of Louisiana. During his stay in Paris, Foulhouze received all the degrees of the AASR, culminating in the 33° on 27 September from the Grand College of Rites of the Grand Orient of France. The speed at which Foulhouze received the degrees is extraordinary and certainly was not normal procedure for the Grand Orient. There is no explanation yet found why this very rare honor was given to such a young Master Mason, nor has the contents of the letter from Preaux ever been revealed. Regardless of what activities Foulhouze later engaged in, he was, in the eyes of the US Masonic community, a legitimate Sovereign Grand Inspector General. Of this event, Foulhouze comments:

> *The Scotch Rite [...] pleased me on account of its truly philosophical principles, and the more I studied it, the more I felt anxious to take its superior degrees, when a fair opportunity so to do offered itself to me in 1845.*
>
> *I was in France, and on the recommendations and letters of my Scotch brothers here, the worshipful Lodge "Clémente Amitié" opened its door to me, and after a short stay among them I was made a Knight R.·. + and a Knight Kadosh, which I am bound to say, rendered still clearer to my eyes and intellect the views which I had long*

entertained on the merits of the Scotch Rite, and forever attached me to its admirable and useful tenets.

The favors thus bestowed on me, were unexpected, and I certainly desired no others, when on a special and unasked resolution of the Supreme Council in the Grand Orient, I was called and raised in that body to the thirty third degree.[21]

Following the death of Grand Commander Jean-Jacques Conte, New Orleans Judge Jean-François Canonge, an influential Past Grand Master of the Grand Lodge of Louisiana, became the Grand Commander of the New Orleans Supreme Council on 20 September 1845. [22] Foulhouze said of Canonge:

As long as he lived, I had but little to do, and contented myself with studying the rite ... [23]

Foulhouze, who had affiliated with the Supreme Council of Louisiana in 1846, was, regardless of his comments, not idle during this period. Foulhouze was appointed Grand Secretary of the Supreme Council of Louisiana in 1847.[24] He, also, advanced through the chairs of Los Amigos del Orden serving as its Worshipful Master in 1847. Once serving his term as Worshipful Master, he was elected a life member of the Grand Lodge. It must also be pointed out that the invasion of the jurisdiction of the Grand Lodge of Louisiana by the Grand Lodge of Mississippi and the creation of the Louisiana Grand Lodge in 1848 would undoubtedly, have occupied a considerable amount of time with all the Worshipful Masters of New Orleans Lodges.

The Grand Lodge of Mississippi and the Union of 1850

A faction within the New Orleans English-speaking York Rite Masons felt that the 1844 Constitution of the Grand Lodge of Louisiana sanctioning the cumulating of the three rites worked by lodges in Louisiana (French, Scottish & York) altered the Grand Lodge into a body that was no longer a true York Rite Grand Lodge.[25] The decision was made by these Masons to sever their association with the Grand Lodge and organize themselves into what they felt was proper York Rite Masonry. A committee was formed, and a letter of grievance was brought before the Grand Lodge of Mississippi on 23 January 1845.[26] The Grand Master of the Grand Lodge of Mississippi was Mexican War hero and former governor of Mississippi, John Anthony Quitman. The Grand Lodge of Mississippi appointed a committee to go to New Orleans to examine the situation. On 21 January 1846, the committee from the Grand Lodge of Mississippi appointed to examine the charges presented by the York Masons from New Orleans presented three reports concerning the events. The first report was presented on behalf of the majority of the committee and concluded that there was "no Grand Lodge of Ancient York Masons within the limits of the State of Louisiana" and that the Grand Lodge of Mississippi had "the power, and it is its duty on proper application, to issue Dispensations and Charters to bodies of Ancient York Masons within the limits of the State of Louisiana, until the constitution of a Grand Lodge within that State."[27] Two "counter" reports were then presented which advised against the Grand Lodge of Mississippi issuing charters within the jurisdiction of the Grand Lodge of Louisiana. The outcome of the events of 21 January (despite the efforts of the two "counter" reports) was the chartering of George Washington Lodge in New Orleans and Lafayette Lodge in Lafayette[28] by the Grand Lodge of Mississippi on 22 February. Relations were severed between the Grand Lodges of Louisiana and Mississippi. The Louisiana Lodges chartered by the Grand Lodge of Mississippi were declared irregular by the Grand Lodge of Louisiana. In total, the Grand Lodge of Mississippi chartered seven Lodges in the New Orleans area by 1848.[29] These seven Lodges united to form the "Louisiana Grand Lodge of Ancient York Masons" on 8 March 1848. The Grand Lodge of Mississippi received an admonishment from most U.S. Grand Lodges, and the majority openly condemned its action.[30] While the future for this splinter group of the Grand Lodge of Louisiana may have looked bleak, several events took place to not only strengthen the position of the English-speaking New Orleans Masons but to assure them of total victory by the loss of French control over almost all forms of Louisiana Masonry.

Jean-François Canonge

One of the last official acts of Grand Commander Jean-François Canonge was a speech made on 3 November 1847 in Baton Rouge in which he is reported as stating that a circular issued by the Mississippi craft lodges in New Orleans was "unworthy of notice."[31] Canonge died on 19 January 1848. On 31 January 1848, James Foulhouze was elected Grand Commander of the New Orleans Supreme Council. The Foulhouze election bypassed several senior members of the Council and clearly, established the popularity of Foulhouze with the Council.

Foulhouze had brought with him various rituals from France[32] which he edited for the New Orleans Council.[33] During the same month as the death of Canonge and the election of Foulhouze, the Charleston Council was taking an action that significantly strengthened its position and further weakened the hold of the French-speaking New Orleans Masons. Albert Mackey (the Grand Secretary of the Charleston Council) sent a notice to the *Freemason's Monthly Magazine* [34] (Boston), which read:

> *At a special session of the Supreme Council ... for the Southern Jurisdiction of the United States of America, our Illustrious Brother, John A. Quitman ... Major General in the Army of the United States, was elected to fill a vacancy in this Supreme Council, and was duly and formally inaugurated a Sovereign Grand Inspector General of the 33d. All Consistories, Councils, Chapters and Lodges under this jurisdiction are hereby ordered to obey and respect him accordingly.*[35]

On 29 January 1849, the Grand Lodge of Louisiana published a report that Foulhouze wrote concerning the cumulation of the rites practiced by the Grand Lodge. On 26 February, the Grand Lodge published Foulhouze's report on the 1833 Concordat. Both reports upheld the positions of the Grand Lodge of Louisiana and encouraged the continued practice of the cumulation of the rites in Louisiana.

On 14 September 1849, Foulhouze and several other New Orleans Masons were honored by Friends of Harmony Lodge (whose Worshipful Master was elder Past Grand Master and Supreme Council of Louisiana Active Member, John Henry Holland) by being made honorary members. An excerpt from the Minutes of the Lodge reads:

> *Whereas by their great ability and impartiality our well beloved Brethren Joseph Walker, Jas. Foulhouze, P. Willman, John D. Kemper & R. Preaux have earned the destination of Honorary Membership, their services in the Masonic vineyard entitling them to some suitable token or tribute of appreciation of their worth, and of the high respect entertained for their estimable personal and Masonic character - they being Brethren to whom a burdened may pour out his sorrows, to whom distress may prefer its suit; Brethren whose hands are guided by justice and whose hearts are expanded by benevolence.*
>
> *Therefore be it now decreed, that the aforesaid distinguished Brethren be and they are hereby created Honorary Members of the Friends of Harmony Lodge of F & A Masons, this as a testimony of regard for the inestimable services as Masons, and their courtesy, affability and kindness as men - well worthy of initiation and the foregoing preamble and resolution being seconded and put is carried unanimously.*[36]

The Union of 1850

The 1848 Louisiana Grand Lodge obtained recognition from only one other Grand Lodge – the Grand Lodge of Mississippi. In 1849, John Gedge, a New Orleans attorney, was elected Grand Master of the Louisiana Grand Lodge. Despite what would seem to be the irregularity of the Louisiana Grand Lodge and the lack of support for this new Grand Lodge within the Masonic community, the Grand Lodge of Louisiana entered into negotiations and finally merged with this body in 1850. The Grand Lodge of Louisiana was left with little choice in this matter. The fact that the Grand Lodge of Louisiana was overwhelmingly considered the "regular" Grand Lodge was not sufficient to overcome the internal problems stemming from the cultural divisions in New Orleans. By mid-1849, it was likely realized that the English-speaking lodges that remained loyal to the Grand Lodge showed signs that continued loyalty would likely not happen. Realizing that the total collapse of the Grand Lodge of Louisiana was a real possibility, the Grand Lodge of Louisiana and the Louisiana Grand Lodge entered into talks designed to merge the two bodies.[37] That merger took place in June of 1850 with the approval of a new Constitution of the Grand Lodge of Louisiana of Free and Accepted Masons. Under the terms of the agreement of the merger, the Louisiana Grand Lodge members became recognized as "regular" by the Grand Lodge of Louisiana. All Lodges chartered by the Louisiana Grand Lodge (or by the Grand Lodge of Mississippi in Louisiana) passed under the jurisdiction of the new Grand Lodge of Louisiana. While the new constitution appeared to merge the two Grand Lodges, the Grand Lodge of Louisiana was, in effect, taken over by the Louisiana Grand Lodge. All non-York Rite Lodges were instructed to turn in their charters to receive York Rite charters from the new Grand Lodge. Three Scottish Rite Lodges, Etoile Polaire, Los Amigos del Orden, and Disciples of the Masonic Senate, sought relief from the *New Orleans Supreme Council*. Of these events, Foulhouze wrote:

> *It was agreed that the Grand Lodge should no more cumulate the rites, that it would have and keep its own forms, but that each Lodge in the East might freely work according to its particular and more favorite rite and tenets.*
>
> *Had that agreement been faithfully observed, another series of quiet days might have ensued in Louisiana: but the newcomers in the Grand Lodge soon showed that far from being sincere, they had crept into our*

> *bosom with the only view to tear it to pieces and to build their powers on the ruins of ours. [...]*
>
> *They made as I had foreseen and foretold, a Constitution by which the Scotch lodges of the East were reduced to naught and the life members of the Grand Lodge expelled from it* [38] *the better to secure the triumph and power of those invaders.*
>
> *But from the moment that the constitution began to work, the Scotch lodges understood their mistake; and not withstanding the blame thrown upon them by the new Grand Lodge which was as it was expected, did not fail to say that they were bound by the vote of the majority at Baton Rouge, they all parted from it, averting and showing that they had been deceived, and could not thus be fetted and annihilated by a paltry trick.*
>
> *That event occasioned a good deal of rumor. The Mississippians who had snatched the power began promulgating their bulls of excommunication. John Gedge, like his imitators of this present Consistory, wrote his reports, made his speeches, sent his circulars, but it was to no purpose.*
>
> *The Supreme Council of Louisiana resumed its authority on the blue lodges of the Scotch rite, and the separation was consummated.*[39]

If the goal of the new 1850 Grand Lodge Constitution and the merger with the Louisiana Grand Lodge was to bring peace to all the Louisiana Masons, it was a total failure. If the goal was to remove the power base in the Grand Lodge from the French-speaking New Orleans Masons, it was a success. The French-speaking New Orleans Masons became split after 1850. Outraged at the turn of events, one faction wished nothing more to do with the Grand Lodge and saw the Supreme Council as the only hope of maintaining the French interests. The other French faction, most likely very tired of the disputes, remained with the Grand Lodge in the hopes of possibly still bringing unity to the troubled Grand Lodge.

The 1850 Union of the Grand Lodge resulted in a perceived need for action in the New Orleans Council. Foulhouze believed he could strengthen the New Orleans Scottish Rite by expanding the number of 33rds in the Council beyond its nine Members. Foulhouze says of this:

Perseverance Lodge #4. Pre-1855 meeting place of the Supreme Council of Louisiana

> *Brother Canonge died and I was elected commander in his place. My first move was to promote to the 33d degree one or two members of each of the lodges then established and of some importance in the city of New Orleans, hoping that their initiation would be the best means to secure the masonic peace in our East, as it would contribute to carry light where it was most needed.* [40]

During Foulhouze's administration of the New Orleans Supreme Council prior to the Concordat, he elevated about 30 Masons to the 33° in the New Orleans Council.[41] Those elevated to the 33rd degree by Foulhouze included Charles Claiborne, Thomas Wharton Collens (22 June 1849), Claude Pierre Samory, and Charles Laffon de Ladébat (11 February 1852). The wisdom of expanding the membership of the Supreme Council was apparently recognized by Albert Pike on 25 March 1859 (Pike's first SC Session as Grand Commander) when he expanded the Membership in the

Charleston Council from nine Members to thirty-three Members.

Charles Claiborne assumed the post of Secretary General for the New Orleans Council, and T. Wharton Collens that of Lt. Grand Commander. The Foulhouze/Collens relationship was a very close one which continued until Foulhouze's death in 1875 – years after both had resigned from Masonry. Foulhouze and Collens would, in the early 1850s, even share a law office.

The Lopez Expedition and James Foulhouze

If the Union of 1850 between the Grand Lodge of Louisiana and the Louisiana Grand Lodge, along with the many bomb shells from that event, were not enough to occupy the minds of the Louisiana Masons, an event took place at the same time that over-shadowed the Masonic events in Louisiana and was thrust into the forefront of the minds and thoughts of most all Americans. This disastrous event directly played a direct part in future New Orleans Masonic "battles."

Narciso Lopez

In 1849 Narciso Lopez, a Venezuelan and former colonel in the Spanish Army, began a campaign to take control of Cuba and replace the Spanish government on the island with his own government. Lopez received limited support from various US politicians but was unable to raise a suitable sized army for his mission. Lopez found better luck in New Orleans, where he raised a small army of about 750 men, mainly veterans of the Mexican War, and sailed out of New Orleans in April of 1850 to capture the island. The mission was a complete failure. The US troops were slaughtered, and Lopez was eventually captured and executed. Reports quickly came to the US and the newspapers of the day reported the "murder" of the US troops along with the capture and execution of not only troops, but vacationing US tourists who happened to be on the island. New Orleans was an obvious "hot spot" for the Lopez Expedition as not only did the expedition leave from New Orleans, but the city contained many Spanish-speaking citizens from Cuba. The Grand Lodge of Louisiana had also chartered two Lodges in Cuba during the early years of the Grand Lodge.[42] The tie between New Orleans and Cuba was close for both the general and Masonic populations.

James Foulhouze became entwined in the Lopez Expedition when he traveled to Cuba at the height of the crisis. A New Orleans newspaper, the *Daily Delta,* ran a story on Foulhouze vehemently criticizing his trip and suggesting that he was, possibly, a spy for the Spanish government.[43] The very evening following the publication of the article concerning Foulhouze, T. Wharton Collens, and Robert Preaux published an article in the *Daily Picayune* explaining that Foulhouze's trip to Cuba was with the goal of, hopefully, securing the release of vacationing US citizens who were caught in the conflict.[44] Foulhouze, being made a Mason in a Spanish-speaking Lodge, had numerous interactions with New Orleans Masons from Cuba. In addition, Foulhouze had gained the confidence of various Spanish officials on the island of Cuba by acting as legal counsel for them several years earlier. Along with the article written by Collens and Preaux, the *Delta* article on Foulhouze received censure from a number of competing New Orleans newspapers. The *Delta* article was exposed to be a newspaper "thriller" story with little basis in fact. One newspaper entitled an article critical of the *Delta's* lack of support for its charges, "Newspaper Intolerance,"[45] and another newspaper calling the event of Foulhouze's trip "A Mission of Humanity."[46] The *Delta* ran one more article in defense of its position, claiming that the matter would be settled when Foulhouze returned to New Orleans and the entire event would be brought to the attention of the public.[47] Nothing more, however, was published on the matter by the *Delta*. The event passed from the public's attention. It was soon realized and attributed to a single newspaper's attempt to sensationalize anything concerning a recent event with the possible goal of increasing its sale of newspapers.

Enter the Charleston Supreme Council

John Gedge, who in 1849 was the Grand Master of the irregular Louisiana Grand Lodge, was elected Grand Master of the Grand Lodge of Louisiana for the year 1851. On 27 March 1851, the Supreme Council of Louisiana issued a manifesto in its own defense. This manifesto examined the New Orleans situation and was an appeal for the establishment of fraternal relations between the Supreme Council of Louisiana and other Masonic Bodies worldwide. With Louisiana Masonry in a state of turmoil and the once influential Supreme Council of Louisiana fighting for order and stability, the time for the Charleston Council to act was at hand.

At the invitation of John Gedge, Albert Mackey came to New Orleans in February of 1852 and established, for the Charleston Council, a Consistory of the 32°. Gedge served as Commander in Chief. The establishment of this Charleston Consistory in New Orleans resulted in a new wave of unrest and paved the way for the Concordat of 1855, merging the Charleston and New Orleans Councils.

The New Orleans Supreme Council responded to the Charleston Consistory in New Orleans by taking several measures. A notice critical of the new consistory was placed in the New Orleans Bee by the New Orleans Supreme Council on 27 February 1852.[48] The notice carried the names of the then 29 Active Members[49] of the New Orleans Council. The Supreme Council of Louisiana also incorporated itself under the official name of "Supreme Council of the Thirty-three [sic] and last degree of the Ancient and Accepted Scotch Rite for the United States of America, sitting at New Orleans, State of Louisiana." The act of incorporation was signed on 7 June 1852 and approved by the Secretary of State, the noted Charles Gayarre, on 13 January 1853.[50]

In July of 1852, Foulhouze traveled to New York to install Henry C. Atwood as Grand Commander of the "Supreme Council of the Thirty-third Degree of and for the Free, Sovereign and Independent State of New York" and then journeyed on to France in an attempt to enlist French support for his cause.

It is noteworthy that Foulhouze at this time embraced the concept that Supreme Councils should be limited to state jurisdictions just as Grand Lodges.[51]

The Concordat of 1855

The speed at which the total loss of the Grand Lodge of Louisiana by the French-speaking Masons occurred caused confusion and uncertainty about their future. James Foulhouze, as Grand Commander of the New Orleans Supreme Council, sought to unite the French-speaking Freemasons under his banner. Whether it was because of the rapid progress of Foulhouze (questions of his competence) or personality conflicts, Foulhouze was unable to unite all the French Masons. The conflict of opinions within the New Orleans Supreme Council as to the direction in which to proceed can reasonably be seen as a contributing factor to the resignation of Foulhouze on 30 July 1853 and nearly all the officers of the Supreme Council of Louisiana by December of 1853. The final break for Foulhouze appears to have occurred at the 22 June meeting of the New Orleans Council. At that meeting, T. Wharton Collens, the Lt. Grand Commander, had prepared a series of resolutions to present to the Council. After a reading of the resolutions, the floor was opened for comment, but instead of addressing the points of the various resolutions, Charles Claiborne apparently began a series of attacks on Foulhouze's clothing. The meeting fell into shouting matches, and the deep-rooted feelings of frustration from the events of the past years seemingly boiled up. Foulhouze, realizing that

T. Wharton Collens

control of the meeting was lost, closed the Council, and departed.[52]

In the absence of the Minutes of the Supreme Council of Louisiana during the Foulhouze years,[53] it can only be presumed that T. Wharton Collens assumed the post of acting Grand Commander for the remainder of 1853 until his own resignation on 19 December of that year. The day following the resignation of Collens, the Grand Treasurer, Jean Baptiste Faget, turned in his letter of resignation, and an undated letter of resignation from Grand Secretary, J.J.E. Massicott, was also accepted by the Council.

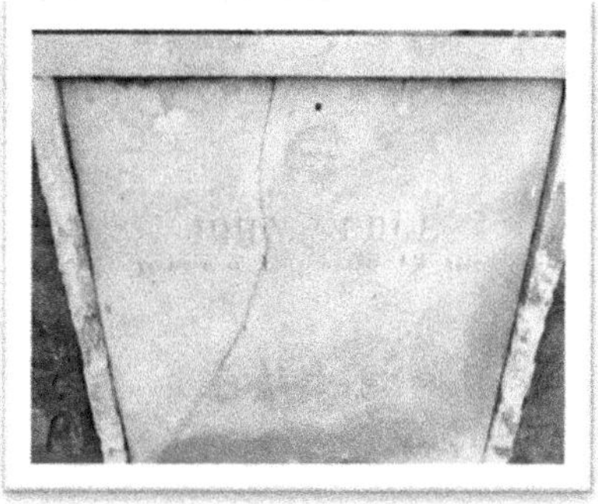

Grave of John Gedge in St. Louis #1 Cemetery

On 7 January 1854, Charles Claiborne was elected Grand Commander of the Supreme Council of Louisiana. Claude Pierre Samory was elected Lt. Grand Commander, and Charles Laffon de Ladébat was appointed Grand Secretary. Samory and Ladébat were part of the French-speaking faction that split from Foulhouze during the 1850-53 turmoil. 1854 was devoted to negotiations with the Charleston Supreme Council. On 6 & 17 February 1855, the concordat merging the New Orleans and Charleston Supreme Councils was signed. Albert Mackey and John Quitman were present in New Orleans for the signing of the Concordat and representing the Charleston Council.

John Gedge, who had spearheaded the drive of the Louisiana Grand Lodge and the 1852 Consistory, did not live to see the concordat between the New Orleans and Charleston Councils – he died on 13 April 1854 during a yellow fever epidemic in New Orleans.

The death of John Gedge must have generated some concern for the future of the newly reorganized Scottish Rite Masonry in New Orleans. Gedge had led a complete and total coup of the Grand Lodge, dramatically altering its nature. It was also Gedge who had written to Mackey to bring a Charleston consistory to New Orleans and took control of it as he did the Grand Lodge. The introduction of the Charleston consistory paved the way for the Concordat of 1855. His influence on the events of the times is unquestionable. It is reasonable to assume that Gedge might have taken some leadership position in the post concordat days had he lived. It is logical that Gedge would have become an Active Member of the Charleston Supreme Council and led the reorganized Grand Consistory of Louisiana. The death of Gedge made this impossible, yet the basic problem remained. An influential figure was needed to lead and unite the fragmented New Orleans Scottish Rite. Regardless of the fact that the Concordat had taken place, there were still quite a number of former Supreme Council of Louisiana 33rds unaffiliated with the Charleston Council – or any Council. The potential for uprising was undeniable. In a letter to Claude Samory, Albert Mackey suggested that the man to lead and unite the New Orleans Scottish Rite Masons had been found, and it was believed that only the formalities remained. Mackey wrote:

> *I hope to be present at the installation of that Bro∴ as S∴G∴I∴G∴ whose adhesion to us will heal all difficulties [...] The moment we receive your nomination, the nominated Bro∴ will be elected.*[54]

The man Mackey wrote of was James Foulhouze. The choosing of Foulhouze to join the Charleston Council and lead the New Orleans Scottish Rite for the Charleston Council is very reasonable and, given the situation, the only logical choice that could be made. Foulhouze was viewed as a regular 33rd from the Grand Orient of France. As Foulhouze was a former Grand Commander of the Supreme Council of Louisiana who resigned before the Concordat, he might have been viewed as a prominent "free agent." The fact that Foulhouze was a member (and even Grand Commander) of the Supreme Council of Louisiana was irrelevant from a regularity standpoint. The matter could be easily settled if he agreed to join the Charleston Council. Samory and Ladébat were also members of the Supreme Council of Louisiana (and both given the 33rd degree by Foulhouze), yet both became Active Members and officers of the Charleston Council. If James Foulhouze agreed to lead the New Orleans Scottish Rite under the Charleston Council banner, the Charleston Council would have a much easier road to travel in bringing the remainder of the New Orleans Scottish Rite Masons under their control. Foulhouze was approached by Albert Mackey and Claude Samory in the summer of 1856 and offered the position of Commander-in-Chief of the Grand Consistory and Active Membership in the Southern Jurisdiction, providing that he joined the Charleston camp.[55] Of this event, Foulhouze wrote:

> *About a year or fifteen months ago, M. Antonio Costa asked me whether I had any objection to converse with M. Claude Samory about the then state of affairs with regard to the Scottish Rite in Louisiana. I answered that I had none. On the following day M. Samory together with M. Costa called on me, and in his presence, told me that he had long been anxious to see me, that he was always my*

friend, that the course which he and other members of the Supreme Council of Louisiana had followed since I left it was with the only view of putting an end to any further contest and quarrel both with the Grand Lodge of our state and the Supreme Council of Charleston, that many a York mason of this east was now initiated to the high degrees of the Scottish Rite, that they all had heard of me as being well versed in its tenets and ceremonies, and were anxious to see me join the Consistory thereto assume the command of the Rite in Louisiana, that indeed I had just cause to complain of the conduct of some BB∴ towards me both in the Supreme Council and in the Polar Star Lodge, but that they all acknowledged it, and were ready on my joining the Grand Consistory, to offer me any apology I might wish, that there was a vacancy in the Supreme Council of Charleston which he had been offered to fill, and which he was ready to give up in my behalf if I would unite with them, that my presence in that Council would do immense good both here and at Charleston, and that the best I could do was to accept, if I desired to carry out my opinion and views with regard to the right which Louisiana has to its Supreme Council.

My answer to M. Samory was as follows:

I need no apology, for any thing which may have been done or said in any masonic body to hurt my feelings. Masonry, thank God, has taught me better desires, and it is enough for me to hear from you that all those who may have had an intention to offend me, do now regret it. As to your proposal, I can in no way or manner accept it. My position is clear and well defined. The Supreme Council of Louisiana was not founded by me. It existed before I was a mason. In 1845 I received, not in the Supreme Council of

France founded by M. Grasse de Tilly, but in the Supreme Council of the Grand Orient, the 33d degree. That most Illustrious body treated me as a future member of the Supreme Council of Louisiana with which it corresponded, and I was commissioned by its Grand Commander and other members to be the interpreter of their good feelings near our Supreme Council. A short time after my return here, our Grand Commander Jean François Canonge died, and I was elected to replace him. On doing so, I bound myself to obey it and protect its rights: and I must say that after a most serious inquiry into its origin and the sources from which it emanates, I am more than ever convinced that my opinion with regard to the fundamental authority of the Scottish Rite is correct, and that the views of Charleston thereon are altogether erroneous. From the moment you and other 33rds of this East judged fit to recognize the Council of Charleston as your superior, I and two other members of our Supreme Council, did immediately exercise what, in such case we considered to be our right, and continued the work of our Supreme Council. It is true that on account of the momentary excitement which has prevailed, we have chosen to be silent, but we exist nevertheless and have resolved to safeguard our power and authority for any case

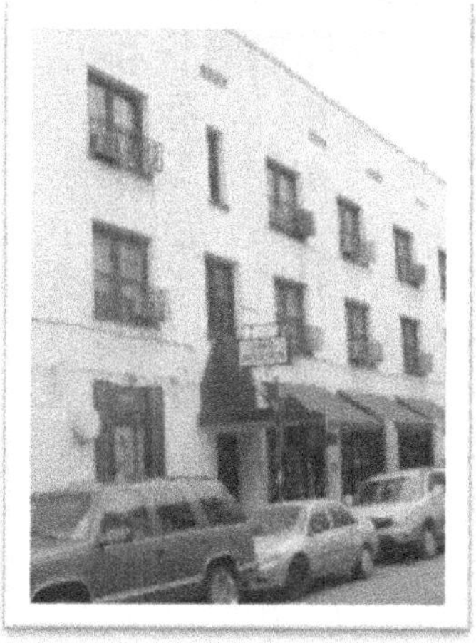

Present day 735 St. Louis Street was the residence of James Foulhouze when he met with Claude Samory and Albert Mackey. Today the building is the home of the Chez Bourbon Apartment Hotel.

of emergency. I certainly feel much honored with the proposition which you make me to accept an appointment as an active member of the Supreme Council of Charleston and as such to preside your Consistory here, but neither such a flattering offer, nor any other consideration can make me deviate from what I consider to be my duty towards a body which I have sworn to protect. I have personally no pretension whatsoever to power. I know that I am good only to make an initiation, and I acknowledge that the privilege of commanding should be better placed in other hands than mine. Many a person, no doubt, will attribute my determination to a spirit of opposition, but as I feel good will towards all and even those who condemn me both in York and Scotish [sic] ranks of Masonry, I will, happen what it may, persevere following the line which I believe to be the only correct one.

Thereupon, M. Samory expressed his hope that I would change my mind, and asked me whether I would like to converse with M. Albert G. Mackey on that subject. I answered affirmatively and two or three days afterward, he called at my house with that Gentleman.

M. Mackey began by expressing a desire that his visit to me should not be considered as official. I replied that being both knights templars, we were authorized to meet as such and talk of the questions relative to the Scotish [sic] Rite, as if we were perfect strangers to it; and it being so agreed, he repeated to me all that M. Samory had said before with regard to the desire expressed by a large number of masons that I should join the consistory, and with regard to my being made an active member of the Council of Charleston and taking as such command of the Scotish rite in Louisiana. I answered him what I had already answered M. Samory. A few words where then exchanged between him and me, with regard to the origin of the council of

Charleston, the constitutions of 1786, the authority which the Supreme Council of the Grand Orient of France claims on the Scotish degrees and the differences which exists between the York and Scotish rites. He admitted that difference and that the reasons which I gave upon all the other points presented a strong matter of consideration, but that he could not accept them as conclusive, which I immediately understood and acknowledged to be with him a matter of course.

He then insisted that I should again consider the proposition made by Mr. C. Samory, and confirmed by himself; and in conclusion he wished me to let him know what my determination would be after more mature reflection.

I promised to do so through Mr. Samory: and this Gentleman having called on me some weeks afterwards, and repeated all that he had been kind enough to say at his first interview with me, I again answered that I could not accept: and I remember having thus addressed him in the end:

'My dear Sir, in the same manner as the masons whom you now represent, express a desire to have me in your Consistory for their best interest, so a time may come when Scotish [sic] masons of this East, tired of a foreign dominion, shall be glad to know that there is in New Orleans a 33d of some value who has never varied, and can at any time be the strong hold around which they may gather as Louisianians.'

Thereon we parted good friends as I parted with Mr. Mackey, after due interchange of kindness and politeness. [56]

In 1858, Charles Laffon de Ladébat, while clearly bitter towards Foulhouze, commented on this meeting between Foulhouze, Samory, and Mackey:

> *Ill Bros. Mackey and Samory knew very well that with a few persons, amoung the weak minded and the ignorant, Mr. Foulhouze was "somebody," and that if they could prevail on him to join the Grand Consistory of Louisiana, peace would be finally restored, and it was solely for the purpose of securing that peace, that they paid him a visit, against the advice of many who knew Mr. Foulhouze better than they.* [57]

Albert Pike

With John Gedge dead and Foulhouze no longer in consideration, Claude Samory became the first New Orleans Mason to be elected an Active member of the Charleston Council. His election was on 20 November 1856. On 17 December 1856, the Grand Consistory filled the vacancy offered to James Foulhouze. The choice was a Mason of promise but little training in the Scottish Rite. The attorney from Arkansas, Albert Pike, was unanimously (and in his absence[58]) elected Commander in Chief of the Grand Consistory of Louisiana.

Prior to the election of both Samory and Pike, James Foulhouze took part in an activity that sealed his fate with the Charleston Council. Foulhouze, along with T.W. Collens, J.J.E. Massicott, J.B. Faget, and other former New Orleans Supreme Council members, declared, in effect, the Concordat of 1855 invalid and publicly resumed the activities of the New Orleans Council. The date that the Supreme Council of Louisiana was re-opened is sometimes disputed. Foulhouze stated in November of 1857:

> *From the moment I had noticed of that nameless act [the Concordat of 1855], I called upon some 33ds, whom I knew to be true to their obligations, and with them I immediately opened the Supreme Council and continued its work, in order that it might not even be said that it had slept a single instant ...* [59]

If such a meeting of 33rds did take place, it was still not until 9 October 1856 that J.J.E. Massicott would be elected Grand Commander of the reorganized Supreme Council of Louisiana, and their activities would become public. That action was the "shot" which started a new round of Masonic turbulence which dramatically altered the nature of the US Scottish Rite.

The Re-origination of the Supreme Council of Louisiana

The days/months/years following the concordat were a time of great uncertainty with many New Orleans Masons. The arguments made by all sounded somewhat reasonable. An examination of who chose to associate with the Charleston Council after the concordat, who chose to associate with the revived Supreme Council of Louisiana, and who chose to associate with neither body provides an interesting look into the divided, confused, and emotional state of affairs. Of the Grand Lodge of Louisiana officers who were Active Members of the Supreme Council of Louisiana in the pre-concordat days, two of the five Past Grand Masters[60] chose to affiliate with neither body. One PGM affiliated with the Charleston

Council[61] and two with the revived New Orleans Council.[62] Of the eight senior Grand Lodge officers, two chose to affiliate with neither body,[63] two with the Charleston Council[64] and four with the revived New Orleans Council.[65] Of the non-Grand Lodge New Orleans 33°s in the pre-concordat days, eight chose to associate with neither body, fifteen with the Charleston Council, and four with the revived New Orleans Council. The total would be: twelve choosing to affiliate with neither body, nineteen with the Charleston Council, and ten with the revived New Orleans Council. These figures should not, however, be viewed as the final tally as they were, over the following years, modified as members moved from one body to the other in a most disconcerting manner. L. E. Deluzain, who was a participant in the 1855 Concordat affiliating with the Charleston Council, re-affiliated with the revived Supreme Council of Louisiana upon its revival. Joseph Lamarre, who was created a 33rd in the revived Supreme Council of Louisiana on 25 February 1858, was tried and expelled by that Council on 22 May 1858. He then affiliated with the Grand Consistory of Louisiana, becoming an Honorary 33rd. Neither side could truly claim clear victory as the severely bitter strife left both sides with ragged edges. Many of those who chose one side or the other eventually retired from any Masonic affiliation.

Possibly concerned over the reorganization of the New Orleans Council, the Grand Consistory of Louisiana sought to organize itself into a state corporation in early 1857. On 19 March 1857, the General Assembly of the Louisiana State Senate and the House of Representatives approved the incorporation of the Grand Consistory of Louisiana. Listed as members were two future Sovereign Grand Commanders of the Charleston Council — Albert Pike and James C. Batchelor.

Pierre Soulé

On 22 April 1857, Foulhouze was elected Grand Commander of the revived New Orleans Council. T. Wharton Collens resumed his former position as Lt. Grand Commander. With Foulhouze back in command, the Supreme Council of Louisiana began to grow in strength and size. 1858 was a pivotal year for Foulhouze and the reorganized New Orleans Supreme Council. In February, Albert Pike delivered a lecture before the Grand Lodge of Louisiana. His lecture was a sharp assault on Foulhouze and the New Orleans Council. The lecture by Pike, and arguments against it, occupied most of the March 1858 issue of the *Masonic Delta.*[66] Without question, the Charleston camp had found a Mason as capable of the "stinging pen" as Foulhouze. February of 1858 also saw a commanding new (really, returning) member to the New Orleans Council. The announcement in the *Masonic Delta* was sure to cause great concern in the Charleston/New Orleans camp:

> *We are happy to say that our most Ill.·. and worthy Bro.·. Pierre Soulé has joined the Supreme Council of the 33d, in and for the Sovereign and Independent State of Louisiana. This eminent citizen and learned Freemason admits thus the State Rights masonically as well as politically.*[67]

The return of this fiery and powerful former United States Senator and US Minister to Spain to the rolls of the Supreme Council of Louisiana was the equivalent of a shot of adrenaline for the New Orleans Council. Soulé was created a 33rd on 8 March 1838 by Jean Jacques Conte and was, actually, a Member of the Supreme Council of Louisiana prior to the election of James Foulhouze as Grand Commander. Soulé apparently resigned from the Council at some point following the election of Foulhouze, as his name is nowhere to be found in any of the records concerning the Concordat of 1855. There is no known record giving the reasons for the resignation of Soulé from the Council nor his Masonic activities during, or thoughts of, the concordat. Soulé was elected a US Senator in 1847 and served in that office until 1853, followed by his appointment as Minister to Spain from 1853-55. Soulé was a vocal, resourceful and respected addition to the New Orleans Council.

The addition of Pierre Soulé as an Active Member of the Supreme Council of Louisiana would seem to be answered one month later by the addition of Albert Pike as an Active Member of the Charleston Council on 20 March 1858.[68] At the very session which elected Pike as an Active Member, Foulhouze was formally "expelled" from the Scottish Rite by the Charleston Council. Since Foulhouze was never a member of any of the bodies controlled by the Charleston Council, this action was more of a public statement of disapproval than an actual expulsion. What followed next was a series of "sledgehammer" verbal and written attacks from and upon both the New Orleans and Charleston Councils. The extremely bitter attacks surpassed even the Cerneau "war," which resulted in the death of all "High Grade" Scottish Rite Masonry in the US, with the exception of New Orleans. Foulhouze released his *Mémoire à Consulter* in French in 1858 and, then, in 1859, issued his *Historical Inquiry into the Origin of the Ancient and Accepted Scottish Rite* in English.[69] The book served as the platform from which Foulhouze stated his case, defined his actions and views on regularity, as well as his concepts of the history of the Scottish Rite. Foulhouze also used the *Masonic Delta* as a platform. This monthly publication was the official organ of the revived Supreme Council of Louisiana. Joseph Lamarre released his *A Masonic Trial in New Orleans* in French in 1858, and Charles Laffon de Ladébat translated and added notes to the work for an English edition. The next major New Orleans Masonic publication was a work designed to answer Foulhouze's *Mémoire à Consulter* and further state the position of the Charleston Council. *A Dissection of the Manifesto of Mr. Charles Bienvenu* was released in 1858 and opened a very regrettable door for the Charleston Council. The work, while originally issued as an anonymous publication, was later learned to be the work of Albert Pike and Charles Laffon de Ladébat. While the *Dissection* was as harsh in tone as Foulhouze's *Mémoire à Consulter*, it went back to the Lopez Expedition period and reprinted at the end of the booklet the article published on Foulhouze by the *Daily Delta* and the retort by T. Wharton Collens and Robert Preaux. What was not published, nor mentioned, was the response of nearly all of the competing New Orleans newspapers condemning the yellow journalistic style of the *Delta's* article on Foulhouze. The illusion created in the *Dissection* was that the *Delta's* article on Foulhouze was factual, and Collens and Preaux were only attempting to deny the obvious. In 1873, James Scot published his *Outline of the Rise and Progress of Freemasonry in Louisiana*. He revealed that the *Dissection* influenced his thinking and beliefs (and assuredly that of many others) of Foulhouze. Scot says of Foulhouze:

> *At this time [1850] he [Foulhouze] was charged with being a spy of the Spanish Government, and was afterwards denounced as such in the newspapers of the day when the news of the fate of the Lopez expedition reached New Orleans. During the excitement he was concealed by some friends to prevent his falling into the hands of the mob, until he was able to effect his escape to Havana. He afterward returned, and resigned his membership in the Supreme Council, July 30, 1853.* [70]

The only newspaper which published such an opinion of Foulhouze was denounced by the balance of the newspapers in New Orleans. Foulhouze went to Havana to secure the release of American citizens *prior* to the article by the *Delta*. He did not "escape" to Havana. The statement by Scot is erroneous and very misleading. James Foulhouze became one who was not viewed as simply holding a very strong opposing Masonic opinion. He was now portrayed as a charlatan and spy of low moral character. It became character assassination. This was quite a different picture than the respected Mason Albert Mackey approached to become an Active Member of the Charleston Council. The Scot quotation is an example of the emotional and confused situation in Louisiana Masonry and that inaccuracies were, sadly, sometimes accepted as fact.

On 3 October 1858, Foulhouze informed the New Orleans Council, in Session, of a communication he received from the Grand Orient of France. Foulhouze, as a Grand Orient 33rd, was officially instructed to disassociate himself from the revived New Orleans Council. Foulhouze refused this mandate. On 4 February 1859, the Grand Orient of France struck Foulhouze's name from its list of 33rds.

Despite the actions taken and the decrees and publications written against Foulhouze and the New Orleans Council, there was no sign that the Council was weakening. In fact, the Supreme Council of Louisiana showed every sign of strengthening. By 1859, the Supreme Council of Louisiana was at its peak of power in the post concordat days. Twenty-five active lodges were under its jurisdiction,[71] and the Council was composed of thirty-four Active Members.[72] Of the lodges under the jurisdiction of the New Orleans Council, seven were located outside of New Orleans in various regions of Louisiana. The makeup of the lodges reveal that the popularity of the Supreme Council of Louisiana was more than just with the French-speaking New Orleans Masons. Twelve lodges worked in the French language, seven in the English language, two in German, one in Italian, and one in Spanish. Remembering that the Louisiana Grand Lodge (with its "irregular" stamp) grew in power and took over the Grand Lodge of Louisiana in 1850 with no outside support, save the Grand Lodge of Mississippi, the matter of the Supreme Council of Louisiana had to be addressed. It was not simply a growing threat to the Charleston Council but also to the Grand Lodge of Louisiana.

With no real structure, rituals, or organization, the Charleston Council apparently began to realize that it was, indeed, in trouble. Of this time Charles S. Lobingier, 33°, G.C. writes in his 1931 *The Supreme Council, 33°*:

> *Both Pike and Mackey had, by this time, decided that the Supreme Council needed reform. On January 20, 1858, the former had written to the latter urging an increase in the membership and the introduction of the elective system.*[73]

For reasons that are, at best, ambiguous, Grand Commander John Honour resigned his office in the Charleston Council on 13 August 1858. It was not until 2 January 1859 that Albert Pike was proclaimed, by Albert Mackey, *elected* to the office of Grand Commander of the Charleston Council. It is logical that the actions of Foulhouze and the Supreme Council of Louisiana influenced the change of command and practice in the Charleston Council. Pike immediately began reforming the Charleston Council and making the necessary changes for its survival.

In 1860, Foulhouze was elected Judge of the Second District Court in Plaquemines Parish. In 1861, Foulhouze moved his domicile from New Orleans to Plaquemines Parish. That same year former judge and Lt. Grand Commander T. Wharton Collens was elected Judge of the Seventh District Court in New Orleans. On 2 January 1861, the Supreme Council of Louisiana re-incorporated itself taking officially, for the first time, the name "The Supreme Council of Louisiana." Due to the pressures of his new legal positions, T.W. Collens resigned in 1861 as Lt. Grand Commander of the New Orleans Council. He was replaced by Sam Brown, who was created a 33rd by Foulhouze on 5 March 1860.

The Civil War

Arguably there has been no lower point in the history of the United States than the Civil War years of 1861-65. The divided country nearly destroyed itself in four years of devastating war, the effects of which plagued the county for a century to follow. While there have been numerous accounts of Masonic acts of charity during the Civil War years, the war weakened

Masonry in the US due to the loss of life, property, and the economic hardship that followed the war years. There is no sign or record that any of the Supreme Councils in the US were active during the Civil Wars years. Pierre Soulé was imprisoned for a time upon the capture of New Orleans in 1862. Upon his release from prison, he lived out the remaining war years in Cuba. Albert Pike was charged with war crimes stemming from the *Battle at Pea Ridge* (his only war command) and was left out of the general amnesty afforded at the close of the war. Pike fled to Canada, awaiting a Presidential pardon allowing him to return to the US.

There are no known records of the Supreme Council of Louisiana during the war years, and it is unknown what events, if any, took place in the Council during this time. James Foulhouze, who prior to the war was a district court judge, is shown after the war as the Parish Attorney for Plaquemines Parish. There are no records of the exact date or reason that he left office as a judge. It is possible that the then 65-year-old Foulhouze retired from his judgeship, or the Union might have required his leaving office in the post war years. A series of events that can best be described as "amazing" then takes place concerning Foulhouze and the New Orleans Council.

On 3 May 1866, T. Wharton Collens, Pierre Soulé, and eight other 33rds of the Supreme Council of Louisiana signed an "oath of allegiance" to the New Orleans Council.[74] Foulhouze's name is not included in this apparent reorganization. On 10 May 1866, the Supreme Council of Louisiana obtained the oath of allegiance of Robert Preaux and created two 33rds. One of the 33rds created was a New Orleans music teacher, music shop owner, and composer of moderate note who corresponded with many of the artistic and literary figures in Europe, including Victor Hugo. His name was Eugene Chassaignac. On 7 January 1867, Chassaignac was elected Grand Commander of the New Orleans Council. It is unknown who was Grand Commander or "acting" Grand Commander at the time that Chassaignac was elevated to the 33rd degree or why Chassaignac was selected to lead the New Orleans Council. There is a full veil of mystery over the election of Chassaignac and the departure of Foulhouze.

The 1 May 1867 minutes of Liberty Lodge #19 (under the New Orleans Council's jurisdiction)[75] show that O.J. Dunn, Grand Master of the Eureka Grand Lodge of Louisiana (Prince Hall) and five other Prince Hall Lodges in various locations in the US had officially accepted the invitation to attend Liberty Lodge and noted that this lodge admitted visitors with no regard to race. The Worshipful Master of Liberty Lodge was Eugene Chassaignac. The New Orleans Council, likewise, and that same year, officially announced that membership to its lodges was not based on race. That announcement seems curious as the Supreme Council of Louisiana (and the whole of New Orleans Masonry) had little concern over race prior to the Civil War.

In an amazing and dramatic move, the Grand Orient of France, ignoring its past action against James Foulhouze, re-recognized the Supreme Council of Louisiana on 5 November 1868. Eugene Chassaignac commented on James Foulhouze and the relations with the Grand Orient of France in the April-May 1869 issue of the *Bulletin:* [76]

> *It is true that in 1858, following the writings of Mr. J. Foulhouze, (writings that were not at all the acts of the Supreme Council) our relations with the Grand Orient were interrupted; but since I have had the honor of being the Grand Commander and Grand Master of the Scotch Rite, in Louisiana, I had the pamphlets disavowed by a solemn resolution; on the other hand, Mr. Foulhouze not being any longer a member of our order, there no longer exists a reason for the relations between the Grand Orient of France and the Supreme Council of Louisiana to be interrupted.*[77]

What could have happened? Without James Foulhouze, the reorganization of the Supreme Council of Louisiana would have failed before it started. The Chassaignac statement can only be viewed as incredible and shows an almost contempt for Foulhouze. Why? There is no clue as to what could have taken place during the Civil War years. Before the war, the Supreme Council of Louisiana was at its height of power. It could have, in a matter of a few years, realistically overpowered the Charleston Council and seriously threatened the Grand Lodge of Louisiana had the war not interrupted its growth. James Foulhouze was the power and the driving force of this movement. It simply could not have happened without him. There is no hint as to why Foulhouze left office, why Chassaignac was made a 33rd, why Chassaignac was elected Grand Commander, or why Chassaignac seemingly turned on Foulhouze. Just as perplexing as the Chassaignac statement on Foulhouze is the re-recognition of the Supreme Council of Louisiana by the Grand Orient. The Grand Orient had stripped Foulhouze of his 33rd Degree for his participation in reorganizing the New Orleans Council. Why would they now recognize that very same Body? The re-recognition of the Supreme Council of

Louisiana by the Grand Orient of France unquestionably caused great concern in the Supreme Councils SJ and NMJ. In a bold move, relations between the Grand Orient and the SJ and NMJ were suspended by a joint resolution of the SJ and NMJ dated 2 May and 15 June 1870. The resolution included the following points (presumably written by Pike).

> *The Grand Orient of France well knew, for it had so decided in a sane interval, in 1858, that an Inspector-General created by itself could exercise no powers within the jurisdiction of another Supreme Council. It knew that the Chassaignac body was created by the sole authority of M. Jacques Foulhouze, whom it had denuded of his privileges as an Inspector-General, for "forfaiture d'honneur," in establishing it. And yet, without any new light upon the subject, without any reconsideration or reexamination, without restoring M. Foulhouze, and while in alliance with us, it recognized this spurious organization as a lawful Supreme Council.* [78]

The Death of James Foulhouze

There is no suggestion found that Foulhouze had any association with Freemasonry following the Civil War years. In 1869 Foulhouze co-authored a book with William M. Prescott titled *The Ordinances of the Police Jury of the Parish of Plaquemines*. Foulhouze is listed as "Parish Attorney" and Prescott as "Parish Judge." Foulhouze apparently busied himself with legal matters and spent the remainder of his life in the river town of Pointe-a-la-Hache, Louisiana.

On 21 December 1875, the following article appeared in the *New Orleans Bee*:

Deceased the 18th of December 1875 at Pointe-a-la- Hache, parish of Plaquemines, the Hon. James Foulhouze at the age of seventy-five. A native of Riom, Auvergue, France.

Headstone of James Foulhouze

Foulhouze was buried at St. Thomas the Apostle Church Cemetery in Pointe-a-la-Hache, Louisiana. T. Wharton Collens, who had resigned from all Masonic activities by then, handled the legal matters concerning Foulhouze's succession. Collens wrote of Foulhouze:

I was very intimately acquainted with the late James Foulhouze during the thirty years that preceded his death. He was a native of Riom in France, and during the thirty years that I knew him he frequently spoke to me of his relatives in that country, and showed me his correspondences with them. His father died previous to 1830, his mother a few years before he 'J. Foulhouze' did. He had a brother who died before he did - that brother left one heir a daughter. Foulhouze himself was never married. [79]

While Foulhouze did not seem to be a man of great wealth, he did own a home in Pointe-a-la-Hache and some property. Foulhouze's entire estate was willed to Odéalie Collens McCaleb, the married daughter of his longtime friend

T. Wharton Collens and Odéalie's son, James Foulhouze McCaleb.

There are many unanswered questions concerning Foulhouze, and the events surrounding him may never be fully answered or understood. It is clear, however, that James Foulhouze followed a path that he felt was correct. Regardless of which side of the issue one takes, it must be objectively recognized that the impact that Foulhouze had on the whole of US Scottish Rite Masonry was substantial. It must also be pointed out that those who supported and held the same opinion as Foulhouze were neither "weak minded" nor "ignorant," as sometimes charged. Intelligent people frequently hold differing opinions. It is unfortunate when judgment is colored by emotion, and it is tragic when erroneous conclusions born of skewed judgment makes its way into accepted history.

Notes:

1. *The Masonic Delta* March 1858.
2. This date was obtained from the tombstone of James Foulhouze located in St. Thomas the Apostle Church Cemetery, Pointe a la Hache, Louisiana.
3. Personal letter: Christine McCullough, Assistant Archivist, Archdiocese of Philadelphia to Michael R. Poll, 23 April 1993.
4. *Passenger and Immigration List Index Vol. I* P. William Filby, Mary K. Meyer Editors. (Detroit, Michigan: Gale Research Co., 1981) 314.
5. Charles Laffon de Ladébat, translator, notes of *A Masonic Trial in New Orleans.* (New Orleans, LA: J. Lamarre, 1858) p. 62.
6. *Encyclopedia Britannica Vol. XI* (Chicago: William Benton, Publisher, 1965) 814.
7. McCullough to Poll, 23 April 1993. It should be noted that a priest having his faculties suspended is akin to a physician having his medical license suspended. The affected priest would no longer be able to carry out the duties of a priest, such as hearing confessions, performing weddings, baptisms, Mass, etc. While a priest who has had his faculties

suspended is prevented from doing all that makes one a priest, only the Vatican can separate a priest from his vows as a priest. This would mean that Foulhouze might have, technically, remained a priest, without powers, until his death.

8. At the time that Foulhouze was a priest, Philadelphia was a "Diocese" and not yet an "Archdiocese."

9. McCullough to Poll, 23 April 1993.

10. Ladébat, notes, *A Masonic Trial in New Orleans* p. 62.

11. James Foulhouze, *A Philosophical Inquiry Respecting the Abolition of Capital Punishment* (New Orleans, LA: Cornerstone Book Publishers, 2019 reprint of 1842 edition.).

12. The paper that Bishop Kenrick mentions was *Le Penseur* (*The Thinker*).

13. *Records of the American Catholic Historical Society Vol. VIII*, 1896 Bishop Kenrick to Dr. Cullen 23 November 1843., 311-312.

14. Masonic and anti-Masonic.

15. *The Louisiana Historical Quarterly Vol. 31, No. 4 October 1948.* New Orleans, LA, 918.

16. Roman Catholic law forbids duels regardless of the fact that, for many years, the traditional site for duels was in the gardens directly behind and on the grounds of the St. Louis Cathedral.

17. *The Masonic Delta* November 1857 edition.

18. Ibid.

19. Ibid.

20. James Foulhouze, *Historical Inquiry into the Origin of the Ancient and Accepted Scottish Rite* (New Orleans, LA: Cornerstone Book Publishers, 2012 reprint of 1859 edition.) 17.

21. *Masonic Delta* November 1857.

22. Canonge served the Grand Lodge of Louisiana as Grand Master in 1822-24 & 1829 and also served as Commander in Chief of the Grand Consistory of Louisiana from 1843-46. Canonge had served as the Grand Senior Warden of the Cerneau Grand Council of Princes of the Royal Secret, 32° in Philadelphia in 1818 and was an early member of the New Orleans Supreme Council, being appointed Grand Expert on 7 November 1839. It was during Canonge's administration as Commander in Chief of the Grand Consistory that this body passed under the jurisdiction of the New Orleans Supreme Council. Prior to his election to the office of Sovereign Grand Commander, Canonge served as the Lt. Grand Commander of the Supreme Council. Canonge had the reputation of being a "no nonsense" and "ready to act" individual with an amazing memory. As a criminal court judge, he once ordered the arrest of the entire

state Supreme Court for interfering in one of his capital trials. *New Orleans Times Democrat* 8 January 1893 "Louisiana Families."

23. *Masonic Delta* November 1857.

24. Foulhouze, *Historical Inquiry* p. 62.

25. See: *The Elimination of the French Influence in Louisiana Masonry,* page 22 of this book.

26. *Report of the Committee on Foreign Correspondence of the Louisiana Grand Lodge of Ancient York Masons.* (New Orleans: Cook, Young & Co., 1849.) 5.

27. Ibid. 5.

28. The town of Lafayette was a suburb of New Orleans in the 1800s, located in what is now considered the "uptown" area of New Orleans.

29. George Washington, Lafayette, Warren, Marion, Crescent City, Hiram & Eureka.

30. *Grand Lodge of the State of Louisiana Report and Exposition* (New Orleans: J.L Sollée, 1849) 5-34.

31. James B. Scot, *Outline of the Rise and Progress of Freemasonry in Louisiana* 1873 (New Orleans, LA: Cornerstone Book Publishers, reprint 2008) 76.

32. Charles Laffon de Ladébat, *Ancient and Accepted Rite. Thirtieth Degree.* (New Orleans: 1857), xxvii.

33. Ladébat states in a footnote of his published 18° ritual: "The philosophical explanation of this and of all the other Degrees from the First up to the Thirtieth inclusive, is taken from the work of Ill.: Bro.: J. Foulhouze, 33d, with some slight alterations, of which, the author willingly assumes the responsibility." Ladébat, *Ancient and Accepted Scotch Rite. Eighteenth Degree* (New Orleans: 1856) 123. Foulhouze had also rewritten the 33° for the New Orleans Council. See: James D. Carter *History of the Supreme Council, 33° SJUSA (1861-1891).* (Washington, DC: The Supreme Council 33°, 1967). 37.

34. The title of this magazine is sometimes given as *Freemasons' Magazine.*

35. Charles S. Lobingier, *The Supreme Council , 33°* (Louisville, KY: The Standard Printing Co., Inc., 1931). 172; Ray Baker Harris, James D. Carter, *History of the Supreme Council, 33° SJUSA (1801-1861),* (Washington, DC: The Supreme Council 33°, 1964.) 236.

36. Minutes Book, Friends of Harmony Lodge #58 14 September 1849.

37. James Scot, *Outline of the Rise and Progress of Freemasonry in Louisiana.* New Orleans, LA: Cornerstone Book Publishers, reprint 2008. 78-80.

38. Prior to the Grand Lodge Constitution of 1850, Past Masters of the constituted lodges were made Life Members of the Grand Lodge with voting rights in the Grand Lodge. Following the Constitution of 1850, voting rights were only given to Grand Lodges Officers, the three

principal members of each lodge, Past Grand Masters, and Grand Lodge Committee members.
39. *The Masonic Delta* November 1857.
40. *The Masonic Delta* November 1857.
41. The numbers vary according to the source. *The Annual Grand Communication of the Supreme Council,* 1859, VIII lists 26 new 33rds. Albert Pike, *Official Bulletin VIII,* 1886, page 571-572 lists 31 new 33rds.
42. Reunion Fraternal de Caridad in Havana 12 July 1815 and El Templo de la Devina Pastora in Matanzaz 12 July 1818, *Proceedings of the Grand Lodge of Louisiana* 1995 (A-2 & 3).
43. *New Orleans Daily Delta* 31 May 1850.
44. *The Daily Picayune,* New Orleans, Louisiana 31 May 1850.
45. *The Daily Crescent* New Orleans, Louisiana 1 June 1850.
46. *Daily Orleanian,* New Orleans, Louisiana 2 June 1850.
47. *New Orleans Daily Delta* 1 June 1850.
48. *New Orleans Bee* 27 February 1852.
49. James Foulhouze, T.W. Collens, Charles Claiborne, J.B. Faget, Felix Garcia, F.A. Lumsden, Joseph Walker, John L. Lewis, Robert Preaux, Charles Murian, S. Heriman, Jean Lamothe, Antonio Costa, A. P. Lanaux, G.A. Montmain, F. Correjolles, J.H. Holland, R.D. Fanis, J.E. Jolly, J. Bachino, Aug. Broué, M. Prados, F. Ricau, J.J.E. Massicott, François Meilleur, C.M. Emerson, H.G. Duvivier, C. Samory & Charles Laffon de Ladebat.
50. *The Masonic Delta* August 1857.
51. An interesting document resides in the New Orleans Scottish Rite Library and Museum. It is a handwritten copy of the 1846 General Regulations of the New Orleans Supreme Council. This document is of particular interest as it was used as a "working copy" for the 1848 General Regulations, which were approved on 20 July 1848. The document contains the notes and changes made by James Foulhouze with his signature. Clearly, the various changes were presented to the Council for approval. The official name "*The Supreme Council for the United States of America Sitting in New Orleans*" at the head of the Regulations has portions scratched out, leaving only "*The Supreme Council sitting in New Orleans.*" In addition, the side margins contain the proposed changes. In addition to the official name being altered to remove "for the United States of America," the proposed change to "for the State of Louisiana" was also scratched out in the margin. Presumably, the new title did not pass the vote of the Council, or Foulhouze decided not to propose this name change – at that time. It is significant, however, to realize that Foulhouze,

from the early days of his administration, considered the Supreme Council structure as possibly being limited to state boundaries just as Grand Lodges.

52. This account cannot be confirmed in totality by any existing official record. But it is recounted in an old unsigned handwritten paper in the New Orleans Scottish Rite Library and Museum. In the notes of the 1859 *A Masonic Trial in New Orleans*, Charles Laffon de Ladébat writes of the event: "*... An opportunity offered and that was the address of Ill.∴ Bro. Chas. Claiborne who, instead of arguing the point at issue, that is, the merits and demerits of the 20 articles, amused himself by ridiculing the masonic costumes of Mr. Foulhouze. Mr. Foulhouze was stung to the quick and swore, in leaving the hall, that he had done with Masonry! He sent in his letter of resignation on the 30th of July 1853.*" P. 43.

53. Alain Bernheim located the Minutes of the New Orleans Supreme Council from its creation to 15 February 1847 in the BN in Paris in 1987. This writer located the Minutes of the New Orleans Supreme Council from the election of Charles Claiborne to the Concordat of 1855 in the Library of the New Orleans Scottish Rite Bodies in 1994.

54. *Official Bulletin VIII* 1886 p 536.

55. Foulhouze, *Historical Inquiry* 78. *The Masonic Delta,* August 1857 & March 1858. Charles Laffon de Ladébat, Translator, *A Masonic Trial in New Orleans (Lamarre's Defense)* (New Orleans, J. Lamarre, 1858) 43-44. Note: *A Masonic Trial in New Orleans* was written by Joseph Lamarre and originally published in French. The work was translated into English and republished that same year. The name of the translator is not given in this work. Charles Laffon de Ladébat states on page 83 of *Dissection of the Manifesto of Mr. Charles Bienienu* (New Orleans: privately published, 1858) that he was the translator for Lamarre's work and author of the notes in that book.

56. *The Masonic Delta* August 1857.

57. Ladébat, *A Masonic Trial in New Orleans* page 43.

58. *Albert Pike's Address Before the Grand Consistory of Louisiana,* page 175 of this book.

59. *The Masonic Delta* November 1857.

60. Felix Garcia, Lucien Hermann.

61. John Henry Holland.

62. Jean Lamothe & Robert Preaux.

63. Ramon Vionnet & Stephen Herriman.

64. François Meilleur and Charles Murian.

65. Jean B. Faget, Jean J.E. Massicott, Romain Brugier and Joseph Lisbony.

66. The revived New Orleans Council's monthly publication.
67. *The Masonic Delta* February 1858.
68. Although Pike was elected an Active Member in March, it was not until 7 July that Mackey would send the official general notification of his election. Harris, Carter *History* 260. Mackey would, however, inform Claude Samory of Pike's election on 8 May 1859. *Official Bulletin VIII*, 544.
69. Foulhouze's *Historical Inquiry* cannot be viewed as an English translation of his *Mémoire à Consulter.* Upon examination by Alain Bernheim, it has been determined that the *Historical Inquiry,* while closely following *Mémoire à Consulter,* has enough significant changes to consider it a rewrite rather than a translation.
70. Scot, *Outline.* 4.
71. *The Masonic Delta* September 1859.
72. The *Masonic Delta* April 1860.
73. Lobingier, *Supreme Council*, 249.
74. Original document in the George Longe Collection in the Amistad Research Center at Tulane University, New Orleans, Louisiana.
75. Photocopy reproduction of the minutes in *The Perfect Ashlar* (current publication of the Supreme Council of Louisiana) October 1969.
76. The *Bulletin* replaced *The Masonic Delta* in 1869 as the official publication of the Supreme Council of Louisiana.
77. Eugene Chassaignac *Bulletin* (New Orleans, A. Simon, 1869) 28.
78. Carter, *History* 431.
79. *Foulhouze Secession Papers,* 1875, Court House Pointe a la Hashe, Louisiana.

MAGVS
V.E.V.

Quantity or Quality?

ONE OF THE GREAT THINGS about living in New Orleans is the food we often take for granted. When I moved back after living away for almost ten years, it was the simple Po-Boy sandwich that gave me such joy. I delighted in finding cozy, hole in the wall places where I could discover new taste sensations. In one such place, I saw a sign advertising the "largest Po-Boy in New Orleans." Well, I had to try this place out. The ad was correct; the sandwich was so big that it really could feed two people with some left over. But, to my great disappointment, it tasted terrible. It was a simple Ham & Swiss, but the cheese was old and hard, and the ham was some sort of nasty discount deli reject. Even the lettuce was soggy and turning brown. It was sure big, but it was a total waste of my money. Clearly, the biggest is not always the best.

I also remember years ago when I first started college. I enrolled at the University of New Orleans (it was then Louisiana State University at New Orleans). I took a civics class, and when I walked in on my first day, it was in an auditorium with something like 300 in the class! I came from a small high school and was overwhelmed. How was I going to learn anything with a sea of people all around me? The following year I transferred to Loyola University in New Orleans and found the class size much more to my liking. In one music class, it was just the instructor and me. That was a learning experience for me. But that's just my taste. The mileage for others may vary.

The fact is that I am more comfortable in small settings. I am more drawn to an intimate, quiet dinner with my wife than dining at the Hard Rock Cafe with a large crowd. But don't misunderstand me. I am all in for a bargain. If that big, ole sandwich had tasted good, I would have been a happy camper. I could have fed my wife and I for the price of one.

The problem with my college civics class was not only huge, but they had not prepared properly. They accepted too many students. Then at the last minute, they realized that too many were in the classroom, so they moved the class to the auditorium. Because of the quick change of venue, they did not think about a microphone. Only a few students sitting in the very front could hear the instructor. They didn't prepare properly. Mistakes were made, and the class suffered.

I am interested in quality experiences. Yes, if all things were equal, I would prefer a small gathering for a quiet dinner. But if the food was bad and the food at the Hard Rock Cafe was outstanding, then the overall winner would be the Hard Rock Cafe. It is no different with Masonry. I want quality, and while I prefer small groups, it should not be understood to mean that I place numbers (large or small) first. I place quality first.

I remember when the big "One Day, All the Way" classes began, and I expressed my concern about them. One argument always seemed to come back at me, which totally missed the point I was trying to make. When I expressed concern about the quality of the events, it would invariably be argued that "bad" degrees were often seen in a small lodge setting. SO WHAT? That's like telling me that eating bad food at a convention center is OK because you can get bad food in a small restaurant! I don't want lousy food anywhere! You can't sell me on something bad because something bad is also offered somewhere else.

A successful lodge can be small or large. It is successful because it does its work properly. And "work" does not just mean ritual. No Worshipful Master should rush into a lodge meeting with no idea of what the secretary will read or announce. The WM should be completely aware of all that will happen in the lodge on any given night. He should also be prepared to manage the occasional unexpected event. In other words, no one would be elected WM of a lodge without spending a good many years in training for the office. Knowing the ritual is only one small part of what is necessary for one to become a successful WM.

A lodge should work as a solid unit. Little groups that develop in Masonic bodies spell death for the body. "I'm in, and you are not" games should have no place in the lodge. The successful lodge moves and acts as one.

It is not the large or small lodge that has any advantage by their number. The lodge with the advantage is the lodge that expects and provides quality work.

MAGVS
V.E.V.

Who Am I?

SOME YEARS BACK, I was visiting my doctor for a check-up. While sitting outside in the waiting room, I picked up a medical magazine and started flipping through it. An article caught my attention. It was titled "Who Am I?" As I started to read it, I became enthralled.

The article told the story of a man in his mid to late 30s who was found by the Chicago police around Midnight on a downtown street. He was unconscious and lying in a pool of blood from an injury to the back of his head. The man was wearing a business suit but had no money, credit cards, or any other identification on him. He was the apparent victim of a mugging.

After spending several days unconscious in the hospital, the man finally awoke. He was completely disoriented. He had no idea how he came to be in the hospital or what might have happened to get him there. As his mind started to clear, instead of an improving situation, things went downhill fast. He began to realize that not only did he not know how he came to be in the hospital, but he also did not know his name, where he was from, or anything at all about himself prior to waking up in the hospital bed. He had complete and total amnesia.

The police sent photos of the injured man to the local media and sent his fingerprints off for possible identification.

Neither proved helpful. Because of the number of large hotels in the area where he was found, the police felt that he could have been a businessman traveling to the city from almost anywhere.

The doctors told the man that amnesia was common with his type of injury. They told him that they could not give any sort of firm prognosis as there was simply too much that was unknown about this type of injury. There was no way to know if all of his memory, some of it, or any of it would return. The doctors also said that they could not give him any sort of time frame on when he might expect to see any changes or improvements. Uncertainty was the only thing of which they were certain.

The man realized that the money and credit cards that were taken from him were insignificant. What they took of true value was his life. If he could not regain his memory, then the man he had been before waking up in the hospital bed was dead.

Think about this man's situation. Each one of us has a personal history in our memories. We remember childhood, family, friends, and happy as well as sad events. We remember school, early jobs, dating, marriage, children, and everything that has gone into shaping us. Who we are today is based, in large part, on the total memory of our experiences. Now, think about all of those memories disappearing into dust in a snap of your fingers. Who would you be? What would you be? How could you be the same person in that situation, and especially if you were alone with no one around who knew you?

This loss of identity and self is not limited to individuals. Groups of people and even whole societies have suffered the same fate. It was known long ago that if one group wanted to defeat another, it was necessary to overpower the enemy's military. But, if one group wanted to completely *destroy* another group, then they would need to wipe out the enemy's history. Look at the Mayans. Their vast library was destroyed, and all their books, save just three, were burned to dust. And what do we know of the Mayan society and people today? What do the decedents of the Mayans know about their own history? Next to nothing.

Even when there was no deliberate attempt at destroying another's history, the lack of history can still create vacuums in our knowledge of the past. In north Louisiana, there is an area known as Poverty Point. There are several large and impressive Indian mounds where a considerable amount of pottery has been excavated. Archaeologists know that this significant civilization existed several thousand years ago and that it is the largest and most complex site of its type discovered in North America. But, because of the lack of any written records and very little information on the people themselves, it is a truly lost society.

Our past is vital to us. The practical reality of the existence and nature of each of us depends on the continued knowledge of our nature and existence. When we die, the continued knowledge of us will only exist if our history is recorded and preserved. If not, then when we die, all knowledge of our achievements, work, *and* who we were dies with us.

Freemasonry is no different. Want to start a debate? Go into any Lodge and ask whether Freemasonry has its roots in the Knights Templar. In some Lodges, such a debate might end up in an argument. The simple truth is that we have little knowledge of the very early history of Freemasonry. The same is pointedly true of the early history of the Scottish Rite. Jurisdictional wars, destruction of early records, and "edited" histories designed to strengthen the argument of one or the other side makes our available knowledge questionable to the objective researcher.

The history of our lodge or other Masonic body should not just be passed off as the concern of "those library types." It is *our* history, and we all share in its proper preservation … or its loss. We need to ensure that proper records are taken and kept and that we take all necessary steps to preserve old documents and records.

When we look at the injured man's situation, we can feel sympathy for him. But we are at best only disinterested parties. We don't know the man, and while we can realize the terrible situation he is in, we do not feel his pain. In Masonry, our loss of history *is* personal. We are not disinterested parties. It is *our* history and *our* personal loss when we are not able to answer questions about ourselves that we should be able to answer. The horrible mistake so many make is in believing that the preservation of our history is someone else's job or duty – as if we play no part in it. If we don't care, we don't exist. It's as simple as that.

What is Truth?

An Address Before the Louisiana Lodge of Research - 02/05/2010

A FEW WEEKS AGO, I tuned in to one of the educational channels on TV and watched a show on archeology. It was an interesting show dealing with the history of archeological practices from the early "Indiana Jones" style to today's standard of documentation. I found a general similarity between the growth and development of archeological excavation standards and those of Masonic research. The show pointed out that in the early days of archeology, researchers would find an important site and break their way in to take whatever they felt was valuable or important. There was little regard for detailed documentation or preservation of the site. Today, great care is taken at excavation sites. It is realized that value and importance are not only with items but where they are located, what might be near them, and the general condition of everything having to do with the site. In the old days of Masonic research, importance was given to special events, but less care was given to verifying the events or knowing what was going on at the time of the event. It is realized today that the whole story, and the understanding of the whole story, entails far more than isolated events.

Technology being developed today is also of great importance to both archeology and Masonic research. Ground penetrating radar allows archeologists to "see" below ground. When these devices are rolled over an area with buried ruins of past civilizations, the whole area becomes visible, and they know where they should begin their dig. In addition, satellites are being employed to help with archeological excavation in overgrown forest areas such as in South America. The satellites are able to filter the forest and discover sites that previously would have been discovered only by rare luck.

Likewise, Masonic research has been greatly aided by advances in technology. Where at one time, a Masonic researcher would need to travel hundreds or thousands of miles to sit in a Masonic library to wade through large stacks of paper documents, today, the computer and internet can put all of the world's great libraries at his fingertips. Databases of information and documents can allow a Masonic researcher to locate, read, and copy documents physically located most anywhere in the world from the researcher's home computer.

While technology allows researchers to locate items of value far more quickly than in past times, the need to understand an item of interest and what it means remains vital. There seems to be a dangerous area between not knowing or caring and truly caring. It is that middle ground where important bits of history are correctly, or more efficiently, discovered but not given the actual proper care that is necessary. Finding an old Masonic diploma means little more than momentary interest if you know nothing of the individual or body for which the diploma was issued. So, is the truth about the importance of an archaeological find depend on our opinion of it? It would seem that once something becomes easier to do, it opens the doors for those with less awareness of actual value or importance to make and then allow carelessness to destroy what is truly important. Or, at least, so it seems. What is the actual truth of the importance of something? How do we know?

During the trial of Jesus, the Roman governor Pontius Pilate asked what would seem to be a straightforward question: "What is truth?" Since that time, philosophers have pondered and debated both the question and its answer – many times with less than satisfactory conclusions.

In the original *Star Wars* movie trilogy of the late 1970s and early 80s, the Jedi Master, Obi-Wan Kenobi, spoke to the young Jedi, Luke Skywalker, about truth. Luke was questioning Obi-Wan about comments that he made about Luke's father that seemed to be untrue. Obi-Wan told him, "Luke, you're going to find that many of the truths we cling to depend greatly upon our own point of view." I needed to think long and hard about that line by Obi-Wan. Maybe sometimes truth, or how we perceive it, is subjective.

In matters of religion, truth does seem to fall very much in line with the thoughts of Obi-Wan. My truth may or may not be your truth. It depends upon our own points of view. How many wars have been fought in the name of religious truth? How many men have been willing to die or kill in the name of religion? How do you prove a religious truth? The poet Kahlil Gibran wrote, "Faith is a knowledge within the heart, beyond the reach of proof." Religious truth is accepted as such simply because we believe it.

In its wisdom, Masonry realized early on that good, honest men could have very different views of religion, politics, or anything – even Freemasonry. As such, pointed religious (or political) discussions are not allowed in the lodge. The outcome of such discussions could result in disharmony. It is the combination of the passion in which a religious or political view is held along with the inability to conclusively prove such views that result in such discussions being emotional powder kegs. One simply does not prove the correctness of a religious view or political opinion in the same manner that they would prove a mathematical equation.

Religion and politics are not the only subjects that can result in passion for a Mason. Masons have a passion for Masonry. Masons very often have a *strong* passion for Masonry. Want to see a good fight? Get two Grand Lecturers together who disagree on whether it should be "on" or "upon." We are taught to subdue our passions, but, truthfully, do we always? So, let's go back to the mid-1800s and keep these thoughts of "passion" and "truth" in our minds.

In New Orleans, the city that care forgot, there were two groups facing off. They differed in language, Masonic customs, Masonic rites, and points of view. They were emotional. They were passionate. They were unyielding. It was not a case of two friends sitting down with one ordering strawberry ice cream and the other chocolate and enjoying each other's company. It was a case of two angry opponents sitting down, disgusted that the other would dare to select a different flavor of ice cream than their flavor. The *truth* held by each was that their *flavor* of Masonry was the best! Period. They were childish. Each group of Masons held to their own "flavor" and would tolerate no difference of opinion as to the validity of their view. It was not even a case of "you are mistaken;" it was a case of "you are a liar." It was a sad, sad time.

The two sides in early New Orleans Masonry refused to bend or try to understand the other. Rather than withdrawing to avoid disharmony, they openly engaged each other in lodge or public settings with bitter and unMasonic attacks upon the character of their brothers. It was a war. It was a nasty war. It was not necessary.

From a strictly historical standpoint, we know some of what took place and some of the "why." But there is much that remains unknown or unclear about the events prior to the "wars." We know but bits and pieces of pre-1850 Louisiana Freemasonry. We have lessons and opportunities.

The lessons should be obvious. We are taught to subdue our passions. We are taught not to speak evil of our brothers – either to their face or by private character assassination. We should try to help each other, not wage war on each other because we have differences of opinion as to the nature of Freemasonry. We should advance the Light of Masonry, not the darkness of ignorance, falsehood, and ambition.

Our opportunities should also be obvious. Never before has technology been available to make the work of Masonic research easier and more possible for anyone with the desire. We have clear standards for conducting, documenting, and presenting our research. We know that we should not present ideas as facts or allow "Masonic politics" to color or sway our research or presentation. We have the chance to do meaningful, objective work that can benefit the Freemasonry of today as well as the future.

The brothers of the mid-1800s were quick to point the finger of blame at "the other guy" for all the perceived wrongs in Masonry during that time. But were the wrongs with Masonry itself or the individual Masons of the time? Was Masonry flawed on either side, or were the individual Masons flawed? Can we see the opportunity to help Masons of today through a study of the unfortunate events of the past?

When our ego allows us to see clearly, we realize that Masonry is better than us. Masonry is not improved because of our membership; *we* are improved because of our membership.

We have an opportunity. We have the tools to do the real work of Masonic research. We have the knowledge to know the nature of the real work of Masonic research. It is up to us to either do that work and earn our keep as Masons or succumb to the three villains.

What is truth? It may depend on what we are made of and our own points of view.

Deadly Apathy

WE HAVE ALL READ or heard stories of individuals who have taken drastic steps to save their own lives. Recently I read of a man who was doing some repair work on his water heater. He needed to reach far into the tank while lying on his back. While working in that position, his arm became wedged in the tank, and he found that it was impossible to remove it. He screamed for help but was alone in the house, and no one was near enough outside to hear his cries. The man had spent several days trapped with his arm hopelessly wedged when he noticed a disturbing smell coming from inside the tank and around his arm. The man later recounted that instinct must have taken over. He managed to reach a saw and began to cut off his arm. The next day, several family members - concerned at not being able to reach him - found him unconscious on the floor in a pool of blood, his arm severed at the elbow. The man was taken to the hospital, where he recovered, but the doctors gave him a sobering report. Gangrene had set into his arm, and he was told that if he had not removed it when he did, he would have died. The doctors also noted that if he had waited any longer to remove the arm, it would have been too late. The poison would have spread through his body, and nothing then would have saved him. The man's life was saved not just because he acted but *when* he took action.

I joined Masonry in the mid-'70s. While a number of my family members had been Masons, I knew next to nothing of the philosophy or history of Freemasonry. All that I knew was that it was a "good" organization. It took my joining to find out what "good" meant. Such ignorance of the philosophy of Freemasonry prior to joining is becoming more of an exception than the rule today. Many of the young men who join Masonry already know much of its philosophy. They have read the popular, new, and exciting books on Freemasonry. They arrive at the door of the Lodge with an awareness of a wonderful, mysterious, moral, and enlightened group of seekers. They want to share in and be a part of such an organization. But, sadly, this is not exactly what they always find when they join.

The numbers of demits, NPD, and non-participation are growing at an alarming rate. The new reports paint a dismal picture. Yes, new members are coming fast, and sometimes in very good numbers, but we seem to be having trouble keeping them. So, why is this happening, and what do we do?

What seems to be happening is the young men come to Freemasonry with an idea of what it should be and find that it is something very different. Many come with the hopes of finding enlightening discussions, intellectual programs designed to lift us to new heights and help to learn more about ourselves and our world. Yet, sometimes all they find are "good ole boys" seeking to add another title, gain a bit more authority or power, and be more of the "big fish" in whatever pond they thrive. There is lots of coffee but little real enlightenment. The young Masons become upset at the reality of their Masonry when they compare it to what they believed of Masonry before they joined. Some make their displeasure known – loudly. At times, such pointed objections by the young brothers are met with disapproval. It is perceived that the young Masons know nothing of what they are talking about, are out of place, and need to "get with the program" and stop "being so negative." The upset young Masons are viewed as the trouble-makers, and their cries for Masonry as they believe it should be are viewed more as the cries of malcontents. They are often ignored and sometimes ostracized. The Masons become disillusioned and wonder why they ever joined.

What happens next takes us back to the man with his arm wedged in the water heater tank. At the moment when he began to smell something very bad, he had a choice. He could act, or he could wait and see. Acting decisively saved his life; waiting to see if the situation changed on its own would have cost him his life. As in many cases, timing is everything. In Freemasonry, our gangrene is apathy. If apathy towards Freemasonry, or any body of Freemasonry, sets into anyone, then they stop caring. Once they stop caring, Masonry does not matter to them, and they turn their back, demit, stop paying their dues, or just live as a card carrier. The positive force that could have been dies. We all lose.

And whose fault is it if a Mason stops caring about Masonry? Suppose we believe or say that it is in some way the fault of the disillusioned Mason, that he would "do better to bring about changes on the inside," or some other such criticism designed to shame him into remaining a member. In that case, we add insult to injury. We have missed the point and are only making a bad situation worse. It would be the same as if we saw the man with his arm wedged in the tank, and we advised him to be patient and hang on a bit longer as things will certainly get better if he just waits out the unpleasant situation. When does "hanging on" reach the point of gangrene and result in death no matter what is done after?

In all cases, objectivity, recognition of the actual situation, and the courage to do what needs to be done must be paramount. If a dedicated, serious Mason ceases to care about some Masonic body, then the "blame game" of identifying who is at fault is pointless. Apathy has won, and Masonry loses.

The time to act is when we see the first signs of actual trouble. The first thing the man with his arm wedged did was try to free his arm. He twisted it, moved it this way and that, and did everything he could to free it. This is the same as if we belong to a dysfunctional Masonic body and we try to suggest ways to improve the body, work for changes and do all we can to correct the situation as a member. If nothing works, then we must take the next step.

When all his own efforts could not free his arm, the man began yelling for help. He could not affect any positive change in the situation; maybe someone else could render him aid. In Masonry, the calling for help would come in the form of seeking out superiors who might be able to correct the situation. When our own best efforts fail, and they sometimes do, we need to seek help from those in a position who might be able to grant what we need.

And what do we do if no help comes? In all cases, we need to act responsibly. We cannot act in haste, foolishly, or without considered thought. But at some point, we need to act. Failure to take any action is often just as reckless and foolish as an action taken too quickly. At some point, the man with his arm wedged knew that something was very wrong. He may not have known all the details or possessed all the medical knowledge of the situation, but he knew that he needed to take drastic action to correct the situation. Oh yes, help did arrive just the next day. But it was too late. Had he waited those additional hours, the poison would have gone through his body, and then nothing would have been able to save him. He took the necessary action, and he took it in time to save his life. He acted.

No one told us that being a Mason was always going to be easy. If someone did, they told us a story. Throughout our degrees, we are given lessons of honor, integrity, and courage. We are given lessons that are sometimes very difficult to put into practice. In my Craft Masonry, we use the Scottish Rite Craft ritual. We are taught that the three "villains" in craft Masonry represent ignorance, falsehood, and ambition. If we have a deficiency of the former or allow any of the latter to gain hold of us, then we do not live Freemasonry as we were taught. Our goal is to control and advance *ourselves*. We must live *our own* lives as Masonry teaches us. We have no control over another, even our closest brother, but we must always have total control over ourselves.

Freemasonry is going through a revolution of sorts. Gone are the days of the "good ole boy" clubs, the power brokers, or the joining of one organization only because it is viewed as a prerequisite for another organization. The young Masons come to us with an understanding of the value of what we teach, not the shiny trinkets we wear. The beauty of what is taught in the various bodies is desired. The leadership of every single body in Masonry must provide quality education, leadership and teach what is supposed to be learned by the new members. If it is in any way unclear as to what is supposed to be taught in any Masonic body, then that should give the clear signal that a change is in order in those bodies. When the ones who must teach don't know themselves, the whole body suffers. Stand up, do the work that you need to do, or allow another to do the work.

Luckily, in many cases, we find that only the first step is necessary for dysfunctional Masonic bodies. We are finding increased cases of the new members realizing that something is very lacking, standing up and taking control of the lacking lodges, and making the positive changes themselves. In those bodies where the membership is not in a position to make such changes on their own authority, then assistance from superiors is necessary, or the body will crumble.

Apathy is the cancer we cannot allow to set into any Mason. Our new, young Masons have a foundation that brings with them hope for our future that is too valuable to ignore. We must do all in our power to see that their interest, dedication, and hunger for Masonry are not trampled by the unworthy or their death grip on their perceived power.

We are in wonderful new times. We must always look to tomorrow if we have any hope of a future than includes Freemasonry.

About The Author

Michael R. Poll (1954 - present) is the owner of Cornerstone Book Publishers and past editor of the *Journal of The Masonic Society*. He is a Fellow and Past President of The Masonic Society, Dean of the Fellows of the Philalethes Society, a Fellow of the Maine Lodge of Research, Member of the Society of Blue Friars, and Full Member of the Texas Lodge of Research.

A New York Times Bestselling writer and publisher, he is a prolific writer, editor, and publisher of Masonic and esoteric books. He is also the host of the YouTube channel "New Orleans Scottish Rite College." As time permits, he travels and speaks on the history of Freemasonry, with a particular focus on the early history of the Scottish Rite.

He was born in New Orleans, LA and lives a peaceful life with his wife and two sons.

MAGVS
V.E.V.

More Masonic Books from Cornerstone

Living Freemasonry
A Better Path to Travel
by Michael R. Poll
6x9 Softcover 180 pages
ISBN 99781934935958

The Particular Nature of Freemasons
by Michael R. Poll
6x9 Softcover 156 pages
ISBN 9781613423462

10,000 Famous Freemasons
4 Vol. Softcover Edition
by William Denslow
Foreword by Harry S. Truman
Cornerstone Foreword by Michael R. Poll
8.5 x 11, Softcover 2 Volumes 1,515 pages
ISBN 1887560319

The Freemason's Monitor
by Thomas Smith Webb
6×9 Softcover 316 pages
ISBN: 1613422717

The Scottish Rite Papers
A Study of the Troubled History of the Louisiana and US Scottish Rite in the Early to Mid-1800s
by Michael R. Poll
6x9 Softcover 240 pages
ISBN 9781613423448

Cornerstone Book Publishers
www.cornerstonepublishers.com

More Masonic Books from Cornerstone

Robert's Rules of Order: Masonic Edition
Revised by Michael R. Poll
6 x 9 Softcover 212 pages
ISBN 1887560076

Seeking Light
The Esoteric Heart of Freemasonry
by Michael R. Poll
6×9 Softcover 156 pages
ISBN: 1613422571

Measured Expectations
The Challenges of Today's Freemasonry
by Michael R. Poll
6×9 Softcover 180 pages
ISBN: 978-1613422946

A Masonic Evolution
The New World of Freemasonry
by Michael R. Poll
6×9 Softcover 176 pages
ISBN: 978-1-61342-315-8

An Encyclopedia of Freemasonry
by Albert Mackey
Revised by William J. Hughan and Edward L. Hawkins
Foreword by Michael R. Poll
8.5 x 11, Softcover 2 Volumes 960 pages
ISBN 1613422520

Cornerstone Book Publishers
www.cornerstonepublishers.com

New Orleans Scottish Rite College

www.youtube.com/c/NewOrleansScottishRiteCollege

Clear, Easy to Watch

Scottish Rite and Craft Lodge

Podcast & Video Education

www.ingramcontent.com/pod-product-compliance
Lightning Source LLC
Chambersburg PA
CBHW031204270326
41931CB00006B/394
9781613421574